George Herber

English Poe

George Herbert

English Poems

ISBN/EAN: 9783744709910

Printed in Europe, USA, Canada, Australia, Japan

Cover: Foto ©Thomas Meinert / pixelio.de

More available books at **www.hansebooks.com**

POEMS AND PROVERBS

OF

George Herbert

Contents

THE TEMPLE

		PAGE
Aaron		183
A Dialogue-Anthem		178
Affliction		42
Affliction		59
Affliction		71
Affliction		89
Affliction		97
Agony, The		32
Altar, The		20
Anagram		76
An Offering		153
Answer, The		177
Antiphon		49
Antiphon		92
A Parody		193
Artillery		144
Assurance		162

		PAGE
A True Hymn	. . . .	176
Avarice	. . . .	75
A Wreath	. . . .	195
Bag, The	. . . .	157
Banquet, The	. . . .	190
Bitter-sweet	. . . .	180
British Church, The	. . . . . .	111
Business	. . . .	114
Call, The	. . . .	163
Charms and Knots	. . . . . .	96
Christmas	. . . .	80
Church Floor, The	. . . . . .	64
Church Lock and Key	. . . . . .	63
Church Monuments	. . . . . .	62
Church Music	. . . .	63
Church Porch, The	. . . . . .	3
Church-Rents and Schisms	. . . . .	145
Clasping of Hands	. . . . . .	164
Collar, The	. . . .	159
Complaining	. . . .	149
Confession	. . . .	129
Conscience	. . . .	106
Constancy	. . . .	70
Coutent	. . . .	66
Cross, The	. . . .	172
Dawning, The	. . . .	113
Death	. . . .	195
Decay	. . . .	99

Contents

vii

PAGE

Dedication, The 1
Denial 78
Dialogue 116
Discharge, The 150
Discipline 188
Divinity 139
Doomsday 196
Dotage 175
Dulness 117
Easter 36
Easter-Wings 38
Elixir, The 194
Employment 54
Employment 77
Even-song 61
Faith 46
Family, The 141
Flower, The 173
Foil, The 185
Forerunners, The 185
Frailty 69
Giddiness 130
Glance, The 180
Glimpse, The 161
Good Friday 33
Grace 57
Grapes, Bunch of the 131
Gratefulness 126

	PAGE
Grief	171
Grieve not the Holy Spirit, &c.	140
Heaven	198
Hold-fast, The	148
Holy Baptism	40
Holy Baptism	40
Holy Communion	48
Holy Scriptures, The	55
Home	108
Hope	124
Humility	68
Invitation, The	189
Jesu	114
Jews, The	159
Jordan	53
Jordan	103
Joseph's Coat	166
Judgement	197
Justice	96
Justice	146
Lent	85
Life	94
Longing	155
Love	50
Love	199
Love-joy	118
Love Unknown	132
Man	90

Contents

	PAGE
Man's Medley	135
Mary Magdalen	182
Mattins	59
Method, The	137
Misery	100
Mortification	98
Nature	41
Obedience	105
Odour, The	184
Our Life is hid with Christ in God	84
Paradise	137
Peace	128
Pearl, The	88
Pilgrimage, The	147
Posy, The	192
Praise	58
Praise	152
Praise	165
Prayer	47
Prayer	104
Priesthood, The	167
Providence	119
Pulley, The	167
Quiddity, The	67
Quip, The	112
Redemption	34
Repentance	44
Reprisal, The	31

		PAGE
Rose, The	. . . .	186
Sacrifice, The	. . . . . .	21
Search, The	. . . .	169
Self-condemnation	. . . . . .	179
Sepulchre	. . . .	35
Sighs and Groans	. . . . . .	82
Sin	. . . .	42
Sin	. . . .	60
Sinner, The	. . . .	32
Sin's round	. . . .	125
Sion	. . . .	107
Size, The	. . . .	142
Son, The	. . . .	176
Star, The	. . . .	72
Storm, The	. . . .	136
Submission	. . . .	95
Sunday	. . . .	73
Superliminare	. . . .	19
Temper, The	. . . .	51
Temper, The	. . . .	52
Thanksgiving, The	. . . . . .	30
Time	. . . .	125
To all Angels and Saints	. . . .	76
Trinity Sunday	. . . .	65
Twenty-third Psalm, The	. . . .	181
Ungratefulness	. . . . . .	81
Unkindness	. . . .	93
Vanity	. . . .	84

Contents

	PAGE
Vanity	113
Virtue	87
Water-course, The	178
Whitsunday	56
Windows, The	65
World, The	83

THE CHURCH MILITANT

The Church Militant	201
L'Envoy	211

MISCELLANEOUS

New Year's Gift to his Mother	215
Inscription in the Parsonage, Bemerton . . .	216
On Lord Danvers	216
A Paradox	217

PROVERBS

Jacula Prudentum, or Outlandish Proverbs, Sentences, &c.	219

The Temple

The Dedication

Lord, my first fruits present themselves to Thee ;
Yet not mine neither : for from Thee they came,
And must return. Accept of them and me,
And make us strive, who shall sing best Thy name.
* Turn their eyes hither, who shall make a gain :*
* Theirs, who shall hurt themselves or me, refrain.*

THE CHURCH PORCH.

PERIRRHANTERIUM.[1]

THOU, whose sweet youth and early hopes enhance
Thy rate and price, and mark thee for a treasure,
Hearken unto a Verser, who may chance
Rhyme thee to good, and make a bait of pleasure:
    A verse may find him who a sermon flies,
    And turn delight into a sacrifice.

Beware of lust; it doth pollute and foul
Whom God in Baptism washed with His own blood:
It blots the lesson written in thy soul;
The holy lines cannot be understood.
    How dare those eyes upon a Bible look,
    Much less towards God, whose lust is all their book!

Wholly abstain, or wed. Thy bounteous Lord
Allows thee choice of paths: take no bye-ways;
But gladly welcome what He doth afford;
Not grudging, that thy lust hath bounds and stays.
    Continence hath his joy: weigh both; and so
    If rottenness have more, let heaven go.

1 [A Greek name for the holy water stoup, or " benatura." See a
reference to it in the second poem, page 19]

If God had laid all common, certainly
Man would have been the encloser: but since now
God hath impaled us, on the contrary
Man breaks the fence, and every ground will plough.
    O what were man, might he himself misplace!
    Sure to be cross he would shift feet and face.

Drink not the third glass, which thou canst not tame,
When once it is within thee; but before
Mayst rule it, as thou list: and pour the shame,
Which it would pour on thee, upon the floor.
    It is most just to throw that on the ground,
    Which would throw me there, if I keep the round.

He that is drunken may his mother kill
Big with his sister: he hath lost the reins,
Is outlawed by himself; all kind of ill
Did with his liquor slide into his veins.
    The drunkard forfeits Man, and doth divest
    All worldly right, save what he hath by beast.

Shall I, to please another's wine-sprung mind
Lose all mine own? God hath given me a measure
Short of his can and body; must I find
A pain in that, wherein he finds a pleasure?
    Stay at the third glass: if thou lose thy hold.
    Then thou art modest, and the wine grows bold.

If reason move not gallants, quit the room;
(All in a shipwreck shift their several way);
Let not a common ruin thee entomb:
Be not a beast in courtesy, but stay,
    Stay at the third cup, or forego the place.
    Wine above all things doth God's stamp deface.

Yet, if thou sin in wine or wantonness,
Boast not thereof; nor make thy shame thy glory.
Frailty gets pardon by submissiveness;
But he that boasts, shuts that out of his story:
   He makes flat war with God, and doth defy
   With his poor clod of earth the spacious sky.

Take not His name, who made thy mouth, in vain:
It gets thee nothing, and hath no excuse.
Lust and wine plead a pleasure, avarice gain :
But the cheap swearer through his open sluice
   Lets his soul run for nought, as little fearing :
   Were I an epicure, I could bate swearing.

When thou dost tell another's jest, therein
Omit the oaths, which true wit cannot need:
Pick out of tales the mirth, but not the sin.
He pares his apple that will cleanly feed.
   Play not away the virtue of that name,
   Which is thy best stake, when griefs make thee tame.

The cheapest sins most dearly punished are;
Because to shun them also is so cheap:
For we have wit to mark them, and to spare.
O crumble not away thy soul's fair heap!
   If thou wilt die, the gates of hell are broad :
   Pride and full sins have made the way a road.

Lie not; but let thy heart be true to God,
Thy mouth to it, thy actions to them both :
Cowards tell lies, and those that fear the rod ;
The stormy working soul spits lies and froth.
   Dare to be true.   Nothing can need a lie :
   A fault, which needs it most, grows two thereby.

Fly idleness, which yet thou canst not fly
By dressing, mistressing, and compliment.
If those take up thy day, the sun will cry
Against thee; for his light was only lent.
    God gave thy soul brave wings; put not those feathers
    Into a bed, to sleep out all ill weathers.

Art thou a magistrate? then be severe:
If studious; copy fair what time hath blurred;
Redeem truth from his jaws: if soldier,
Chase brave employments with a naked sword
    Throughout the world. Fool not; for all may have,
    If they dare try, a glorious life, or grave.

O England! full of sin, but most of sloth!
Spit out thy phlegm, and fill thy breast with glory:
Thy gentry bleats, as if thy native cloth
Transfused a sheepishness into thy story:
    Not that they all are so; but that the most
    Are gone to grass, and in the pasture lost.

This loss springs chiefly from our education.
Some till their ground, but let weeds choke their son:
Some mark a partridge, never their child's fashion:
Some ship them over, and the thing is done.
    Study this art, make it thy great design;
    And if God's image move thee not, let thine.

Some great estates provide, but do not breed
A mastering mind; so both are lost thereby:
Or else they breed them tender, make them need
All that they leave: this is flat poverty.
    For he that needs five thousand pound to live,
    Is full as poor as he that needs but five.

The way to make thy son rich, is to fill
His mind with rest, before his trunk with riches:
For wealth without contentment, climbs a hill,
To feel those tempests, which fly over ditches.
  But if thy son can make ten pound his measure,
  Then all thou addest may be called his treasure.

When thou dost purpose ought (within thy power)
Be sure to do it, though it be but small:
Constancy knits the bones, and makes us stour
When wanton pleasures beckon us to thrall.
  Who breaks his own bond, forfeiteth himself:
  What nature made a ship, he makes a shelf.

Do all things like a man, not sneakingly:
Think the king sees thee still; for his King does.
Simpering is but a lay-hypocrisy:
Give it a corner, and the clue undoes.
  Who fears to do ill, sets himself a task:
  Who fears to do well, sure should wear a mask.

Look to thy mouth: diseases enter there.
Thou hast two sconces, if thy stomach call;
Carve, or discourse; do not a famine fear.
Who carves, is kind to two; who talks, to all.
  Look on meat, think it dirt, then eat a bit;
  And say withal, *Earth to earth I commit.*

Slight those who say amidst their sickly healths,
Thou livest by rule. What doth not so but man?
Houses are built by rule, and commonwealths.
Entice the trusty sun, if that you can,
  From his ecliptic line; beckon the sky.
  Who lives by rule then, keeps good company.

Who keeps no guard upon himself, is slack,
And rots to nothing at the next great thaw.
Man is a shop of rules, a well-trussed pack,
Whose every parcel underwrites a law.
    Lose not thyself, nor give thy humours way :
    God gave them to thee under lock and key.

By all means use sometimes to be alone.
Salute thyself : see what thy soul doth wear.
Dare to look in thy chest ; for 'tis thine own :
And tumble up and down what thou find'st there.
    Who cannot rest till he good fellows find,
    He breaks up house, turns out of doors his mind.

Be thrifty, but not covetous : therefore give
Thy need, thine honour, and thy friend his due.
Never was scraper brave man.   Get to live ;
Then live, and use it : else, it is not true
    That thou hast gotten.   Surely use alone
    Makes money not a contemptible stone.

Never exceed thy income.   Youth may make
Even with the year : but age, if it will hit,
Shoots a bow short, and lessens still his stake,
As the day lessens, and his life with it.
    Thy children, kindred, friends upon thee call ;
    Before thy journey fairly part with all.

Yet in thy thriving still misdoubt some evil ;
Lest gaining gain on thee, and make thee dim
To all things else.   Wealth is the conjurer's devil ;
Whom when he thinks he hath, the devil hath him.
    Gold thou mayst safely touch ; but if it stick
    Unto thy hands, it woundeth to the quick.

What skills it, if a bag of stones or gold
About thy neck do drown thee? raise thy head;
Take stars for money; stars not to be told
By any art, yet to be purchased.
   ·None is so wasteful as the scraping dame;
    She loseth three for one; her soul, rest, fame.

By no means run in debt: take thine own measure.
Who cannot live on twenty pound a year,
Cannot on forty: he's a man of pleasure,
A kind of thing that's for itself too dear.
   The curious unthrift makes his clothes too wide,
    And spares himself, but would his tailor chide.

Spend not on hopes. They that by pleading clothes
Do fortunes seek, when worth and service fail,
Would have their tale believed for their oaths,
And are like empty vessels under sail.
   Old courtiers know this; therefore set out so,
    As all the day thou mayst hold out to go.

In clothes, cheap handsomeness doth bear the bell.
Wisdom's a trimmer thing, than shop e'er gave.
Say not then, This with that lace will do well;
But, This with my discretion will be brave.
   Much curiousness is a perpetual wooing,
    Nothing with labour, folly long a doing.

Play not for gain, but sport. Who plays for more,
Than he can lose with pleasure, stakes his heart:
Perhaps his wife's too, and whom she hath bore;
Servants and churches also play their part.
   Only a herald, who that way doth pass,   [glass.
    Finds his cracked name at length in the Church-

If yet thou love game at so dear a rate,
Learn this, that hath old gamesters dearly cost :
Dost lose ? rise up : dost win ? rise in that state.
Who strive to sit out losing hands, are lost.
     Game is a civil gunpowder, in peace
     Blowing up houses with their whole increase.

In conversation boldness now bears sway.
But know, that nothing can so foolish be,
As empty boldness : therefore first assay
To stuff thy mind with solid bravery ;
     Then march on gallant : get substantial worth :
     Boldness gilds finely, and will set it forth.

Be sweet to all.   Is thy complexion sour?
Then keep such company ; make them thine allay :
Get a sharp wife, a servant that will lour.
A stumbler stumbles least in rugged way.
     Command thyself in chief.   He life's war knows,
     Whom all his passions follow as he goes.

Catch not at quarrels.   He that dares not speak
Plainly and home, is coward of the two.
Think not thy fame at every twitch will break :
By great deeds show that thou canst little do ;
     And do them not : that shall thy wisdom be ;
     And change thy temperance into bravery.

If that thy fame with every toy be posed,
'Tis a thin web, which poisonous fancies make ;
But the great soldier's honour was composed
Of thicker stuff, which would endure a shake.
     Wisdom picks friends ; civility plays the rest.
     A toy shunn'd cleanly passeth with the best.

Laugh not too much : the witty man laughs least :
For wit is news only to ignorance.
Less at thine own things laugh ; lest in the jest
Thy person share, and the conceit advance.
    Make not thy sport, abuses : for the fly,
    That feeds on dung, is coloured thereby.

Pick out of mirth, like stones out of thy ground,
Profaneness, filthiness, abusiveness.
These are the scum with which coarse wits abound :
The fine may spare these well, yet not go less.
    All things are big with jest : nothing that's plain
    But may be witty, if thou hast the vein.

Wit's an unruly engine, wildly striking
Sometimes a friend, sometimes the engineer :
Hast thou the knack ? pamper it not with liking :
But if thou want it, buy it not too dear.
    Many affecting wit beyond their power,
    Have got to be a dear fool for an hour.

A sad wise valour is the brave complexion,
That leads the van, and swallows up the cities.
The giggler is a milkmaid, whom infection,
Or a fired beacon frighteth from his ditties.
    Then he's the sport : the mirth then in him rests,
    And the sad man is cock of all his jests.

Towards great persons use respective boldness :
That temper gives them theirs, and yet doth take
Nothing from thine : in service, care or coldness
Doth ratably thy fortunes mar or make.
    Feed no man in his sins : for adulation
    Doth make thee parcel-devil in damnation.

Envy not greatness : for thou mak'st thereby
Thyself the worse, and so the distance greater.
Be not thine own worm : yet such jealousy,
As hurts not others, but may make thee better,
   Is a good spur.   Correct thy passion's spite ;
   Then may the beasts draw thee to happy light.

When baseness is exalted, do not bate
The place its honour for the person's sake.
The shrine is that which thou dost venerate ;
And not the beast that bears it on his back.
   I care not though the cloth of state should be
   Not of rich arras, but mean tapestry.

Thy friend put in thy bosom : wear his eyes
Still in thy heart, that he may see what's there.
If cause require, thou art his sacrifice ;
Thy drops of blood must pay down all his fear ;
   But love is lost ; the way of friendship's gone ;
   Though David had his Jonathan, Christ his John.

Yet be not surety, if thou be a father.
Love is a personal debt.   I cannot give
My children's right, nor ought he take it : rather
Both friends should die, than hinder them to live.
   Fathers first enter bonds to nature's ends ;
   And are her sureties, ere they are a friend's.

If thou be single, all thy goods and ground
Submit to love ; but yet not more than all.
Give one estate, as one life.   None is bound
To work for two, who brought himself to thrall.
   God made me one man ; love makes me no more,
   Till labour come, and make my weakness score.

In thy discourse, if thou desire to please;
All such is courteous, useful, new, or witty:
Usefulness comes by labour, wit by ease;
Courtesy grows in court; news in the city.
  Get a good stock of these, then draw the card;
  That suits him best, of whom thy speech is heard.

Entice all neatly to what they know best;
For so thou dost thyself and him a pleasure:
(But a proud ignorance will lose his rest,
Rather than show his cards); steal from his treasure
  What to ask farther. · Doubts well-raised do lock
  The speaker to thee, and preserve thy stock.

If thou be master-gunner, spend not all
That thou canst speak, at once; but husband it,
And give men turns of speech: do not forestall
By lavishness thine own, and other's wit,
  As if thou madest thy will. A civil guest
  Will no more talk all, than eat all the feast.

Be calm in arguing: for fierceness makes
Error a fault, and truth discourtesy.
Why should I feel another man's mistakes
More than his sicknesses or poverty?
  In love I should: but anger is not love,
  Nor wisdom neither; therefore gently move.

Calmness is great advantage: he that lets
Another chafe, may warm him at his fire:
Mark all his wanderings, and enjoy his frets;
As cunning fencers suffer heat to tire.
  Truth dwells not in the clouds: the bow that's there
  Doth often aim at, never hit the sphere.

Mark what another says: for many are
Full of themselves, and answer their own notion.
Take all into thee; then with equal care
Balance each dram of reason, like a potion.
   If truth be with thy friend, be with them both:
   Share in the conquest, and confess a troth.

Be useful where thou livest, that they may
Both want, and wish thy pleasing presence still.
Kindness, good parts, great places, are the way
To compass this. Find out men's wants and will,
   And meet them there. All worldly joys go less
   To the one joy of doing kindnesses.

Pitch thy behaviour low, thy projects high;
So shalt thou humble and magnanimous be:
Sink not in spirit: who aimeth at the sky
Shoots higher much than he that means a tree.
   A grain of glory mixt with humbleness
   Cures both a fever and lethargicness.

Let thy mind still be bent, still plotting where,
And when, and how the business may be done.
Slackness breeds worms; but the sure traveller,
Though he alight sometimes, still goeth on.
   Active and stirring spirits live alone:
   Write on the others, *Here lies such a one.*

Slight not the smallest loss, whether it be
In love or honour; take account of all:
Shine like the sun in every corner: see
Whether thy stock of credit swell, or fall.
   Who say, *I care not*, those I give for lost;
   And to instruct them, 'twill not quit the cost.

Scorn no man's love, though of a mean degree;
(Love is a present for a mighty king,)
Much less make any one thine enemy.
As guns destroy, so may a little sling.
   The cunning workman never doth refuse
   The meanest tool that he may chance to use.

All foreign wisdom doth amount to this,
To take all that is given; whether wealth,
Or love, or language; nothing comes amiss:
A good digestion turneth all to health:
   And then, as far as fair behaviour may,
   Strike off all scores; none are so clear as they.

Keep all thy native good, and naturalize
All foreign of that name; but scorn their ill:
Embrace their activeness, not vanities.
Who follows all things, forfeiteth his will.
   If thou observest strangers in each fit,
   In time they'll run thee out of all thy wit.

Affect in things about thee cleanliness,
That all may gladly board thee, as a flower.
Slovens take up their stock of noisomeness
Beforehand, and anticipate their last hour.
   Let thy mind's sweetness have his operation
   Upon thy body, clothes, and habitation.

In alms regard thy means, and others' merit.
Think Heaven a better bargain, than to give
Only thy single market-money for it.
Join hands with God to make a man to live.
   Give to all something; to a good poor man,
   Till thou change names, and be where he began.

Man is God's image; but a poor man is
Christ's stamp to boot: both images regard.
God reckons for him, counts the favour His:
Write, *So much given to God;* thou shalt be heard.
    Let thy alms go before, and keep heaven's gate
    Open for thee; or both may come too late.

Restore to God His due in tithe and time:
A tithe purloined cankers the whole estate.
Sundays observe: think when the bells do chime,
'Tis angels' music; therefore come not late.
    God then deals blessings: if a king did so,
    Who would not haste, nay give, to see the show?

Twice on the day His due is understood;
For all the week thy food so oft He gave thee.
Thy cheer is mended; bate not of the food,
Because 'tis better, and perhaps may save thee.
    Thwart not th' Almighty God: O be not cross.
    Fast when thou wilt; but then 'tis gain, not loss.

Though private prayer be a brave design,
Yet public hath more promises, more love:
And love's a weight to hearts, to eyes a sign.
We all are but cold suitors; let us move
    Where it is warmest. Leave thy six and seven;
    Pray with the most: for where most pray, is heaven.

When once thy foot enters the church, be bare.
God is more there, than thou: for thou art there
Only by His permission. Then beware,
And make thyself all reverence and fear.
    Kneeling ne'er spoiled silk stockings: quit thy state.
    All equal are within the church's gate.

Resort to sermons, but to prayers most:
Praying's the end of preaching.   O be drest;
Stay not for the other pin: why thou hast lost
A joy for it worth worlds.   Thus hell doth jest
   Away thy blessings, and extremely flout thee,
   Thy clothes being fast, but thy soul loose about thee.

In time of service seal up both thine eyes,
And send them to thy heart: that, spying sin,
They may weep out the stains by them did rise:
Those doors being shut, all by the ear comes in.
   Who marks in church-time others' symmetry,
   Makes all their beauty his deformity.

Let vain or busy thoughts have there no part:
Bring not thy plough, thy plots, thy pleasures thither.
Christ purged His temple ; so must thou thy heart.
All worldly thoughts are but thieves met together
   To cozen thee.   Look to thy actions well;
   For Churches either are our Heaven or Hell.

Judge not the preacher; for he is thy judge :
If thou mislike him, thou conceiv'st him not.
God calleth preaching folly.   Do not grudge
To pick out treasures from an earthen pot.
   The worst speak something good if all want sense,
   God takes a text, and preacheth patience.

He that gets patience, and the blessing which
Preachers conclude with, hath not lost his pains.
He that by being at church escapes the ditch,
Which he might fall in by companions, gains.
   He that loves God's abode, and to combine
   With saints on earth, shall one day with them shine.

Jest not at preachers' language, or expression :
How know'st thou, but thy sins made him miscarry?
Then turn thy faults and his into confession :
God sent him, whatsoe'er he be : O tarry,
    And love him for his Master: his condition,
    Though it be ill, makes him no ill physician.

None shall in hell such bitter pangs endure
As those, who mock at God's way of salvation.
Whom oil and balsams kill, what salve can cure ?
They drink with greediness a full damnation.
    The Jews refused thunder; and we, folly !
    Though God do hedge us in, yet who is holy?

Sum up at night what thou hast done by day ;
And in the morning, what thou hast to do.
Dress and undress thy soul : mark the decay
And growth of it : if with thy watch, that too
    Be down, then wind up both ; since we shall be
    Most surely judged, make thy accounts agree.

In brief, acquit thee bravely ; play the man.
Look not on pleasures as they come, but go.
Defer not the least virtue : life's poor span
Make not an ell, by trifling in thy woe.
    If thou do ill, the joy fades, not the pains :
    If well ; the pain doth fade, the joy remains.

SUPERLIMINARE

THOU, whom the former precepts have
   Sprinkled, and taught how to behave
Thyself in church ; approach, and taste
The Church's mystical repast.

Avoid profaneness ; come not here :
Nothing but holy, pure, and clear,
Or that which groaneth to be so,
May at his peril further go.

THE ALTAR

A BROKEN ALTAR, Lord, Thy servant rears,
   Made of a heart, and cemented with tears:
Whose parts are as Thy hand did frame;
No workman's tool hath touched the
       same.

    A   HEART   alone
    Is   such   a   stone,
    As   nothing   but
    Thy power doth cut.
    Wherefore each part
    Of my hard heart
    Meets in this frame,
    To praise Thy name:

That, if I chance to hold my peace,
These stones to praise Thee may not
       cease.
O let Thy blessed SACRIFICE be mine,
And sanctify this ALTAR to be Thine.

THE SACRIFICE

O ALL ye, who pass by, whose eyes and mind
To worldly things are sharp, but to Me blind;
To Me, who took eyes that I might you find:
Was ever grief like Mine?

The princes of My people make a head
Against their Maker: they do wish Me dead,
Who cannot wish, except I give them bread:
Was ever grief like Mine?

Without Me each one, who doth now Me brave,
Had to this day been an Egyptian slave.
They use that power against Me, which I gave:
Was ever grief like Mine?

Mine own apostle, who the bag did bear,
Though he had all I had, did not forbear
To sell Me also, and to put Me there:
Was ever grief like Mine?

For thirty pence he did My death devise,
Who at three hundred did the ointment prize,
Not half so sweet as My sweet sacrifice:
Was ever grief like Mine?

Therefore My soul melts, and My heart's dear treasure
Drops blood (the only beads) my words to measure:
O let this cup pass, if it be Thy pleasure:
Was ever grief like Mine?

These drops being tempered with a sinner's tears,
A balsam are for both the hemispheres,
Curing all wounds, but Mine; all, but My fears.
Was ever grief like Mine?

Yet My disciples sleep : I cannot gain
One hour of watching ; but their drowsy brain
Comforts not Me, and doth My doctrine stain ;
Was ever grief like Mine ?

Arise, arise, they come.   Look how they run !
Alas ! what haste they make to be undone !
How with their lanterns do they seek the Sun !
Was ever grief like Mine ?

With clubs and staves they seek Me, as a thief,
Who am the way of truth, the true relief,
Most true to those who are My greatest grief :
Was ever grief like Mine ?

Judas, dost thou betray Me with a kiss ?
Canst thou find hell about My lips ? and miss
Of life, just at the gates of life and bliss ?
Was ever grief like Mine ?

See, they lay hold on Me, not with the hands
Of faith, but fury ; yet at their commands
I suffer binding, Who have loosed their bands :
Was ever grief like Mine ?

All My disciples fly ; fear puts a bar
Betwixt My friends and Me.   They leave the star,
That brought the wise men of the East from far :
Was ever grief like Mine ?

Then from one ruler to another bound
They lead Me : urging, that it was not sound
What I taught : comments would the text confound.
Was ever grief like Mine ?

The priests and rulers all false witness seek
'Gainst Him, who seeks not life, but is the meek
And ready Paschal Lamb of this great week :
Was ever grief like Mine?

Then they accuse Me of great blasphemy,
That I did thrust into the Deity,
Who never thought that any robbery :
Was ever grief like Mine?

Some said, that I the temple to the floor
In three days razed, and raised as before.
Why, He that built the world can do much more :
Was ever grief like Mine?

Then they condemn Me all with that same breath,
Which I do give them daily, unto death.
Thus Adam My first breathing rendereth :
Was ever grief like Mine?

They bind, and lead Me unto Herod : he
Sends Me to Pilate. This makes them agree ;
But yet their friendship is My enmity.
Was ever grief like Mine?

Herod and all his bands do set Me light,
Who teach all hands to war, fingers to fight,
And only am the Lord of hosts and might.
Was ever grief like Mine?

Herod in judgment sits, while I do stand ;
Examines me with a censorious hand :
I him obey, who all things else command :
Was ever grief like Mine?

The Jews accuse Me with despitefulness;
And vying malice with My gentleness,
Pick quarrels with their only happiness :
              Was ever grief like Mine ?

I answer nothing, but with patience prove
If stony hearts will melt with gentle love.
But who does hawk at eagles with a dove?
              Was ever grief like Mine ?

My silence rather doth augment their cry ;
My Dove doth back into My bosom fly,
Because the raging waters still are high :
              Was ever grief like Mine ?

Hark how they cry aloud still, *Crucify :*
It is not fit He live a day, they cry,
Who cannot live less than eternally ·
              Was ever grief like Mine ?

Pilate, a stranger, holdeth off; but they,
Mine own dear people, cry, *Away, away,*
With noises confused frighting the day :
              Was ever grief like Mine ?

Yet still they shout, and cry, and stop their ears,
Putting My life among their sins and fears,
And therefore wish *My blood on them and theirs.*
              Was ever grief like Mine ?

See how spite cankers things.   These words aright
Used, and wished, are the whole world's delight :
But honey is their gall, brightness their night :
              Was ever grief like Mine ?

They choose a murderer, and all agree
In him to do themselves a courtesy;
For it was their own cause who killed Me:
   Was ever grief like Mine?

And a seditious murderer he was:
But I the Prince of peace; peace that doth pass
All understanding, more than heaven doth glass:
   Was ever grief like Mine?

Why, Cæsar is their only King, not I:
He clave the stony rock, when they were dry;
But surely not their hearts, as I well try:
   Was ever grief like Mine?

Ah, how they scourge Me! yet My tenderness
Doubles each lash . and yet their bitterness
Winds up My grief to a mysteriousness:
   Was ever grief like Mine?

They buffet Me, and box Me as they list,
Who grasp the earth and heaven with My fist,
And never yet, whom I would punish, missed:
   Was ever grief like Mine?

Behold, they spit on Me in scornful wise;
Who by My spittle gave the blind man eyes,
Leaving his blindness to Mine enemies:
   Was ever grief like Mine?

My face they cover, though it be divine.
As Moses' face was veilèd, so is Mine,
Lest on their double-dark souls either shine:
   Was ever grief like Mine?

Servants and abjects flout Me ; they are witty :
Now prophesy who strikes Thee! is their ditty.
So they, in Me, deny themselves all pity ·
        Was ever grief like Mine?

And now I am delivered unto death,
Which each one calls for so with utmost breath,
That he before Me well-nigh suffereth :
        Was ever grief like Mine?

Weep not, dear friends, since I for both have wept,
When all My tears were blood, the while you slept :
Your tears for your own fortunes should be kept :
        Was ever grief like Mine?

The soldiers lead Me to the common hall ;
There they deride Me, they abuse Me all :
Yet for twelve heavenly legions I could call :
        Was ever grief like Mine?

Then with a scarlet robe they Me array ;
Which shews My blood to be the only way,
And cordial left to repair man's decay :
        Was ever grief like Mine?

Then on My head a crown of thorns I wear ;
For these are all the grapes Sion doth bear,
Though I My vine planted and watered there :
        Was ever grief like Mine?

So sits the earth's great curse in Adam's fall
Upon My head : so I remove it all
From the earth unto My brows, and bear the thrall :
        Was ever grief like Mine?

Then with the reed they gave to Me before,
They strike My head, the Rock from whence all store
Of heavenly blessings issue evermore:
            Was ever grief like Mine?

They bow their knees to Me, and cry, *Hail, King:*
Whatever scoffs or scornfulness can bring,
I am the floor, the sink, where they it fling:
            Was ever grief like Mine?

Yet since man's sceptres are as frail as reeds,
And thorny all their crowns, bloody their weeds;
I, who am Truth, turn into truth their deeds:
            Was ever grief like Mine?

The soldiers also spit upon that face
Which angels did desire to have the grace,
And prophets once to see, but found no place:
            Was ever grief like Mine?

Thus trimmed forth they bring Me to the rout,
Who *Crucify Him,* cry with one strong shout.
God holds His peace at man, and man cries out:
            Was ever grief like Mine?

They lead Me in once more, and putting then
My own clothes on, they lead Me out again.
Whom devils fly, thus is He tossed of men:
            Was ever grief like Mine?

And now weary of sport, glad to engross
All spite in one, counting My life their loss,
They carry me to My most bitter cross:
            Was ever grief like Mine?

My cross I bear Myself, until I faint:
Then Simon bears it for Me by constraint,
The decreed burden of each mortal Saint:
  Was ever grief like Mine?

O all ye who pass by, behold and see:
Man stole the fruit, but I must climb the tree;
The tree of life to all, but only Me:
  Was ever grief like Mine?

Lo, here I hang, charged with a world of sin,
The greater world o' the two; for that came in
By words, but this by sorrow I must win:
  Was ever grief like Mine?

Such sorrow, as if sinful man could feel,
Or feel his part, he would not cease to kneel,
Till all were melted, though he were all steel.
  Was ever grief like Mine?

But, *O My God, My God!* why leav'st Thou Me,
The Son, in Whom Thou dost delight to be?
My God, My God————
  Never was grief like Mine.

Shame tears My soul, My body many a wound;
Sharp nails pierce this, but sharper that confound;
Reproaches, which are free, while I am bound:
  Was ever grief like Mine?

Now heal Thyself, Physician; now come down.
Alas! I did so, when I left My crown
And Father's smile for you, to feel His frown:
  Was ever grief like Mine?

In healing not Myself, there doth consist
All that salvation, which ye now resist ;
Your safety in My sickness doth subsist :
      Was ever grief like Mine?

Betwixt two thieves I spend My utmost breath,
As he that for some robbery suffereth.
Alas ! what have I stolen from you? death:
      Was ever grief like Mine?

A King my title is, prefixed on high ;
Yet by My subjects I'm condemned to die
A servile death in servile company :
      Was ever grief like Mine?

They give Me vinegar mingled with gall,
But more with malice : yet, when they did call,
With manna, Angel's food, I fed them all :
      Was ever grief like Mine?

They part My garments, and by lot dispose
My coat, the type of love, which once cured those
Who sought for help, never malicious foes :
      Was ever grief like Mine?

Nay, after death their spite shall further go ;
For they will pierce My side, I full well know ;
That as sin came, so Sacraments might flow :
      Was ever grief like Mine?

But now I die ; now all is finished.
My woe, man's weal : and now I bow My head :
Only let others say, when I am dead,
      Never was grief like Mine!

THE THANKSGIVING

O KING of grief! (a title strange, yet true,
   To Thee of all Kings only due)
O King of wounds! how shall I grieve for Thee,
   Who in all grief preventest me?
Shall I weep blood? why, Thou hast wept such store,
   That all Thy body was one door.
Shall I be scourged, flouted, boxed, sold?
   'Tis but to tell the tale is told.
My God, My God, why dost Thou part from Me?
   Was such a grief as cannot be.
Shall I then sing, skipping Thy doleful story,
   And side with Thy triumphant glory?
Shall Thy strokes be my stroking? thorns, my flower?
   Thy rod, my posy? cross, my bower?
But how then shall I imitate Thee, and
   Copy Thy fair, though bloody hand?
Surely I will revenge me on Thy love,
   And try who shall victorious prove.
If Thou dost give me wealth; I will restore
   All back unto Thee by the poor.
If Thou dost give me honour; men shall see,
   The honour doth belong to Thee.
I will not marry; or, if she be mine,
   She and her children shall be Thine.
My bosom-friend if he blaspheme Thy name,
   I will tear thence his love and fame.
One half of me being gone, the rest I give
   Unto some chapel, die or live.
As for Thy passion—but of that anon,
   When with the other I have done.
For Thy predestination, I'll contrive,
   That three years hence, if I survive,

I'll build a spital, or mend common ways,
     But mend my own without delays.
Then I will use the works of Thy creation,
     As if I used them but for fashion.
The world and I will quarrel; and the year
     Shall not perceive, that I am here.
My music shall find Thee, and every string
     Shall have his attribute to sing;
That altogether may accord in Thee,
     And prove one God, one harmony.
If Thou shalt give me wit, it shall appear,
     If Thou hast given it me, 'tis here.
Nay, I will read Thy book, and never move
     Till I have found therein Thy love;
Thy art of love, which I'll turn back on Thee,
     O my dear Saviour, Victory!
Then for Thy passion—I will do for that—
     Alas, my God, I know not what.

THE REPRISAL

I HAVE considered it, and find
   There is no dealing with Thy mighty passion:
For though I die for Thee, I am behind;
    My sins deserve the condemnation.

    O make me innocent, that I
May give a disentangled state and free;
And yet Thy wounds still my attempts defy,
    For by Thy death I die for Thee.

    Ah! was it not enough that Thou
By Thy eternal glory didst outgo me?
Couldst Thou not grief's sad conquests me allow,
    But in all victories overthrow me?

Yet by confession will I come
Into the conquest. Though I can do nought
Against Thee, in Thee I will overcome
    The man, who once against Thee fought.

.

THE AGONY

PHILOSOPHERS have measured mountains,
    Fathomed the depths of seas, of states, and kings,
Walked with a staff to heaven, and traced fountains:
    But there are two vast, spacious things,
The which to measure it doth more behove :
Yet few there are that sound them; sin and love.

Who would know sin, let him repair
Unto mount Olivet; there shall he see
A Man so wrung with pains, that all His hair,
    His skin, His garments, bloody be.
Sin is that press and vice, which forceth pain
To hunt his cruel food through every vein.

Who knows not love, let him assay,
And taste that juice, which on the cross a pike
Did set again abroach; then let him say
    If ever he did taste the like.
Love is that liquor sweet and most divine,
Which my God feels as blood; but I, as wine.

.

THE SINNER

LORD, how am I all ague, when I seek
    What I have treasured in my memory !
    Since, if my soul make even with the week,
Each seventh note by right is due to Thee.

I find there quarries of piled vanities,
   But shreds of holiness, that dare not venture
   To show their face, since cross to Thy decrees:
There the circumference earth is, heaven the centre.
In so much dregs the quintessence is small:
   The spirit and good extract of my heart
   Comes to about the many hundredth part.
Yet, Lord, restore Thy image, hear my call:
   And though my hard heart scarce to Thee can
      groan,
   Remember that Thou once didst write in stone.

GOOD FRIDAY

O MY chief good,
   How shall I measure out Thy blood?
How shall I count what Thee befell,
   And each grief tell?

Shall I Thy woes
Number according to Thy foes?
Or, since one star showed Thy first breath,
   Shall all Thy death?

Or shall each leaf,
Which falls in autumn, score a grief?
Or cannot leaves, but fruit, be sign
   Of the true vine?

Then let each hour
Of my whole life one grief devour;
That Thy distress through all may run,
   And be my sun.

c

Or rather let
My several sins their sorrows get;
That, as each beast his cure doth know,
Each sin may so.

SINCE blood is fittest, Lord, to write
Thy sorrows in, and bloody fight;
My heart hath store; write there, where in
One box doth lie both ink and sin:

That when sin spies so many foes,
Thy whips, Thy nails, Thy wounds, Thy woes,
All come to lodge there, sin may say,
No room for me, and fly away.

Sin being gone, oh fill the place
And keep possession with Thy grace;
Lest sin take courage and return,
And all the writings blot or burn.

REDEMPTION

HAVING been tenant long to a rich Lord,
Not thriving, I resolved to be bold,
And make a suit unto Him, to afford
A new small-rented lease, and cancel the old.

In heaven at His manor I Him sought.
They told me there, that He was lately gone
About some land, which He had dearly bought
Long since on earth, to take possession.

I straight returned, and knowing His great birth,
   Sought Him accordingly in great resorts;
   In cities, theatres, gardens, parks, and courts:
At length I heard a ragged noise and mirth
   Of thieves and murderers: there I Him espied,
   Who straight, *Your suit is granted*, said, and died.

SEPULCHRE

O BLESSED Body! whither art Thou thrown?
   No lodging for Thee, but a cold hard stone?
So many hearts on earth, and yet not one
          Receive Thee?

Sure there is room within our hearts good store;
For they can lodge transgressions by the score:
Thousands of toys dwell there, yet out of door
          They leave Thee.

But that which shews them large, shews them unfit.
Whatever sin did this pure rock commit,
Which holds Thee now? Who hath indited it
          Of murder?

Where our hard hearts have took up stones to brain
   Thee,
And missing this, most falsely did arraign Thee;
Only these stones in quiet entertain Thee,
          And order.

And as of old, the law by heavenly art
Was writ in stone; so Thou, which also art
The letter of the word, find'st no fit heart
                         To hold Thee.

Yet do we still persist as we began,
And so should perish, but that nothing can,
Though it be cold, hard, foul, from loving man
                         Withhold Thee.

EASTER

RISE heart; thy Lord is risen. Sing His praise
                         Without delays,
Who takes thee by the hand, that thou likewise
                         With Him mayst rise:
That, as His death calcinèd thee to dust,
His life may make thee gold, and much more, just.

Awake, my lute, and struggle for thy part
                         With all thy art.
The cross taught all wood to resound His name
                         Who bore the same.
His stretched sinews taught all strings what key
Is best to celebrate this most high day.

Consort both heart and lute, and twist a song
                         Pleasant and long:
Or.since all music is but three parts vied,
                         And multiplied;
O let Thy blessed Spirit bear a part,
And make up our defects with His sweet art.

I GOT me flowers to strew Thy way;
I got me boughs off many a tree:
But Thou wast up by break of day,
And brought'st Thy sweets along with Thee.

The sun arising in the east,
Though he give light, and the east perfume;
If they should offer to contest
With Thy arising, they presume.

Can there be any day but this,
Though many suns to shine endeavour?
We count three hundred, but we miss:
There is but one, and that one ever.

EASTER

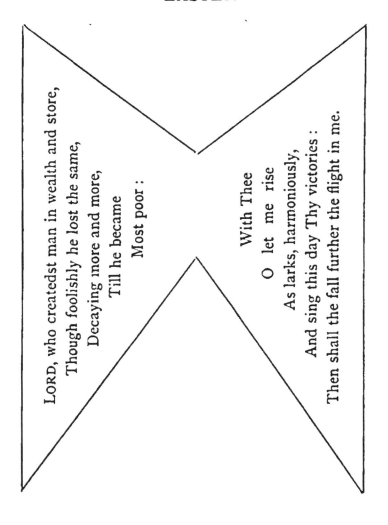

LORD, who createdst man in wealth and store,
Though foolishly he lost the same,
Decaying more and more,
Till he became
Most poor :

With Thee
O let me rise
As larks, harmoniously,
And sing this day Thy victories :
Then shall the fall further the flight in me.

WINGS

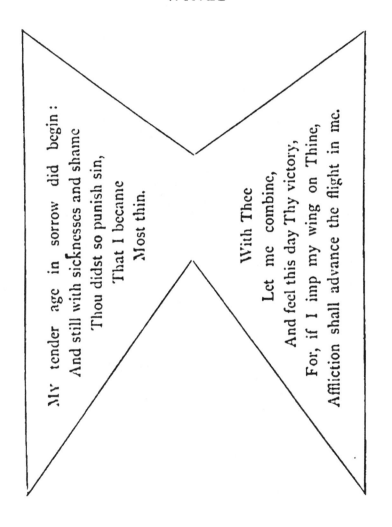

My tender age in sorrow did begin :
And still with sicknesses and shame
Thou didst so punish sin,
That I became
Most thin.

With Thee
Let me combine,
And feel this day Thy victory,
For, if I imp my wing on Thine,
Affliction shall advance the flight in me.

HOLY BAPTISM

A S he that sees a dark and shady grove,
      Stays not, but looks beyond it on the sky;
   So when I view my sins, mine eyes remove
More backward still, and to that water fly,

Which is above the heavens, whose spring and vent
      Is in my dear Redeemer's pierced side.
      O blessed streams! either ye do prevent
And stop our sins from growing thick and wide,

Or else give tears to drown them, as they grow.
      In you Redemption measures all my time,
      And spreads the plaster equal to the crime:
You taught the book of life my name, that so,

   Whatever future sins should me miscall,
   Your first acquaintance might discredit all.

HOLY BAPTISM

S INCE, Lord, to Thee
      A narrow way and little gate
Is all the passage, on my infancy
      Thou didst lay hold, and antedate
      My faith in me.

      O let me still
      Write Thee great God, and me a child:
Let me be soft and supple to Thy will,
      Small to myself, to others mild,
      Behither ill.

Although by stealth
My flesh get on; yet let her sister,
My soul, bid nothing, but preserve her wealth:
The growth of flesh is but a blister;
Childhood is health.

NATURE

FULL of rebellion, I would die,
  Or fight, or travel, or deny,
That Thou hast ought to do with me.
                O tame my heart;
                It is Thy highest art
To captivate strong holds to Thee.

If Thou shalt let this venom lurk,
And in suggestions fume and work,
My soul will turn to bubbles straight,
                And thence by kind
                Vanish into a wind,
Making Thy workmanship deceit.

O smooth my rugged heart, and there
Engrave Thy reverend law and fear;
Or make a new one, since the old
                Is sapless grown,
                And a much fitter stone
To hide my dust, than Thee to hold.

SIN

L ORD, with what care hast Thou begirt us round!
    Parents first season us: then schoolmasters
      Deliver us to laws; they send us bound
To rules of reason, holy messengers,

Pulpits and Sundays, sorrow dogging sin,
    Afflictions sorted, anguish of all sizes,
      Fine nets and stratagems to catch us in,
Bibles laid open, millions of surprises,

Blessings beforehand, ties of gratefulness,
    The sound of glory ringing in our ears;
      Without, our shame; within, our consciences;
Angels and grace, eternal hopes and fears.

    Yet all these fences and their whole array
    One cunning bosom-sin blows quite away.

AFFLICTION

W HEN first Thou didst entice to Thee my heart,
      I thought the service brave:
So many joys I writ down for my part,
      Besides what I might have
Out of my stock of natural delights,
Augmented with Thy gracious benefits.

I lookèd on Thy furniture so fine,
      And made it fine to me,
Thy glorious household-stuff did me entwine,
      And 'tice me unto Thee.
Such stars I counted mine: both heaven and earth
Paid me my wages in a world of mirth.

What pleasures could I want, whose King I served,
         Where joys my fellows were?
Thus argued into hopes, my thoughts reserved
         No place for grief or fear;
Therefore my sudden soul caught at the place,
And made her youth and fierceness seek Thy face:

At first Thou gav'st me milk and sweetnesses;
         I had my wish and way:
My days were strewed with flowers and happiness:
         There was no month but May.
But with my years sorrow did twist and grow,
And made a party unawares for woe.

My flesh began unto my soul in pain,
         Sicknesses cleave my bones,
Consuming agues dwell in every vein,
         And tune my breath to groans:
Sorrow was all my soul; I scarce believed,
Till grief did tell me roundly, that I lived.

When I got health, Thou took'st away my life,
         And more; for my friends die;
My mirth and edge was lost; a blunted knife
         Was of more use than I.
Thus thin and lean without a fence or friend,
I was blown through with every storm and wind.

Whereas my birth and spirit rather took
         The way that takes the town;
Thou didst betray me to a lingering book,
         And wrap me in a gown.
I was entangled in the world of strife,
Before I had the power to change my life.

Yet, for I threatened oft the siege to raise,
         Not simpering all mine age,
Thou often didst with academic praise
         Melt and disolve my rage.
I took Thy sweetened pill, till I came near;
I could not go away, nor persevere.

Yet lest perchance I should too happy be
         In my unhappiness,
Turning my purge to food, Thou throwest me
         Into more sicknesses.
Thus doth Thy power cross-bias me, not making
Thine own gift good, yet me from my ways taking.

Now I am here, what Thou wilt do with me
         None of my books will show:
I read, and sigh, and wish I were a tree;
         For sure then I should grow
To fruit or shade: at least some bird would trust
Her household to me, and I should be just.

Yet, though Thou troublest me, I must be meek;
         In weakness must be stout;
Well, I will change the service, and go seek
         Some other master out.
Ah, my dear God! though I am clean forgot,
Let me not love Thee, if I love Thee not.

REPENTANCE

LORD, I confess my sin is great:
    Great is my sin. O! gently treat
With Thy quick flower, Thy momentary bloom;
         Whose life still pressing
         Is one undressing,
    A steady aiming at a tomb.

Man's age is two hours' work, or three;
Each day doth round about us see.
Thus are we to delights: but we are all
 To sorrows old,
 If life be told
From what life feeleth, Adam's fall.

O let Thy height of mercy then
Compassionate short-breathèd men,
Cut me not off for my most foul transgression:
 I do confess
 My foolishness:
My God, accept of my confession.

Sweeten at length this bitter bowl,
Which Thou hast poured into my soul;
Thy wormwood turn to health, winds to fair weather:
 For if Thou stay,
 I and this day,
As we did rise, we die together.

When Thou for sin rebukest man,
Forthwith he waxeth woe and wan:
Bitterness fills our bowels; all our hearts
 Pine, and decay,
 And drop away, ·
And carry with them the other parts.

But Thou wilt sin and grief destroy;
That so the broken bones may joy,
And tune together in a well-set song,
 Full of His praises
 Who dead men raises.
Fractures well cured make us more strong.

FAITH

LORD, how couldst Thou so much appease
  Thy wrath for sin, as when man's sight was dim,
And could see little, to regard his ease,
    And bring by Faith all things to him?

    Hungry I was, and had no meat:
I did conceit a most delicious feast;
I had it straight, and did as truly eat,
    As ever did a welcome guest.

    There is a rare outlandish root,
Which when I could not get, I thought it here:
That apprehension cured so well my foot,
    That I can walk to heaven well near.

    I owed thousands and much more:
I did believe that I did nothing owe,
And lived accordingly; my creditor
    Believes so too, and lets me go.

    Faith makes me anything, or all
That I believe is in the sacred story:
And when sin placeth me in Adam's fall,
    Faith sets me higher in his glory.

    If I go lower in the book
What can be lower than the common manger?
Faith puts me there with Him, who sweetly took
    Our flesh and frailty, death and danger.

    If bliss had lien in art or strength,
None but the wise and strong had gained it:
Where now by Faith all arms are of a length;
    One size doth all conditions fit.

A peasant may believe as much
As a great clerk, and reach the highest stature.
Thus dost Thou make proud knowledge bend and
    crouch,
    While grace fills up uneven nature.

When creatures had no real light
Inherent in them, Thou didst make the sun,
Impute a lustre, and allow them bright:
    And in this shew what Christ hath done.

That which before was darkened clean
With bushy groves, pricking the looker's eye,
Vanished away, when Faith did change the scene:
    And then appeared a glorious sky.

What though my body run to dust?
Faith cleaves unto it, counting every grain,
With an exact and most particular trust,
    Reserving all for flesh again.

PRAYER ✓

PRAYER, the Church's banquet, Angel's age,
  God's breath in man returning to his birth,
    The soul in paraphrase, heart in pilgrimage,
The Christian plummet sounding heaven and earth;

Engine against the Almighty, sinner's tower,
    Reversed thunder, Christ-side-piercing spear,
    The six-days' world-transposing in an hour,
A kind of tune, which all things hear and fear;

Softness, and peace, and joy, and love, and bliss,
 Exalted manna, gladness of the best,
 Heaven in ordinary, man well drest,
The milky way, the bird of Paradise,

 Church-bells beyond the stars heard, the soul's
  blood,
 The land of spices, something understood.

HOLY COMMUNION

NOT in rich furniture, or fine array,
 Nor in a wedge of gold,
 Thou, who from me wast sold,
To me dost now Thyself convey;
For so Thou shouldst without me still have been,
 Leaving within me sin:

But by the way of nourishment and strength,
 Thou creep'st into my breast;
 Making Thy way my rest,
And Thy small quantities my length;
Which spread their forces into every part,
 Meeting sin's force and art.

Yet can these not get over to my soul,
 Leaping the wall that parts
 Our souls and fleshly hearts;
 But as th' out-works, they may control
My rebel-flesh, and, carrying Thy name,
 Affright both sin and shame.

Only Thy grace, which with these elements comes,
    Knoweth the ready way,
    And hath the privy key,
  Opening the soul's most subtile rooms :
While those to spirits refined, at door attend
    Despatches from their friend.

GIVE me my captive soul, or take
    My body also thither.
Another lift like this will make
    Them both to be together.

Before that sin turned flesh to stone,
    And all our lump to leaven ;
A fervent sigh might well have blown
    Our innocent earth to heaven.

For sure when Adam did not know
    To sin, or sin to smother ;
He might to heaven from Paradise go,
    As from one room to another.

Thou hast restored us to this ease
    By this Thy heavenly blood,
Which I can go to, when I please,
    And leave the earth to their food.

ANTIPHON

Cho.   LET all the world in every corner sing,
                My God and King.

  Vers. The heavens are not too high,
     His praise may thither fly :
     The earth is not too low,
     His praises there may grow.

Cho. Let all the world in every corner sing,
    My God and King.

Vers. The Church with psalms must shout,
    No door can keep them out:
    But above all, the heart
    Must bear the longest part.

Cho. Let all the world in every corner sing,
    My God and King.

⌐ L O V E

PART I.

IMMORTAL Love, author of this great frame,
  Sprung from that beauty which can never fade;
  How hath man parcelled out thy glorious name,
And thrown it on that dust which thou hast made,

While mortal love doth all the title gain!
  Which siding with invention, they together
  Bear all the sway, possessing heart and brain,
(Thy workmanship) and give thee share in neither.

Wit fancies beauty, beauty raiseth wit:
  The world is theirs; they two play out the game,
  Thou standing by: and though thy glorious name
Wrought out deliverance from the infernal pit,

Who sings thy praise? only a scarf or glove
Doth warm our hands, and make them write of love,

PART II.

IMMORTAL Heat, O let thy greater flame
  Attract the lesser to it: let those fires
  Which shall consume the world, first make it tame,
And kindle in our hearts such true desires,

As may consume our lusts, and make thee way.
  Then shall our hearts pant thee; then shall our
  All her inventions on thine altar lay,   [brain
And there in hymns send back thy fire again:

Our eyes shall see thee, which before saw dust;
  Dust blown by wit, till that they both were blind:
  Thou shalt recover all thy goods in kind,
Who wert disseized by usurping lust:

  All knees shall bow to thee; all wits shall rise,
  And praise Him who did make and mend our eyes.

THE TEMPER

HOW should I praise Thee, Lord! how should
   my rhymes
  Gladly engrave Thy love in steel,
  If what my soul doth feel sometimes,
    My soul might ever feel!

Although there were some forty heavens, or more,
  Sometimes I peer above them all;
  Sometimes I hardly reach a score,
    Sometimes to hell I fall.

O rack me not to such a vast extent;
   Those distances belong to Thee:
   The world's too little for Thy tent,
      A grave too big for me.

Wilt Thou meet arms with man, that Thou dost stretch
   A crumb of dust from heaven to hell?
   Will great God measure with a wretch?
      Shall he Thy stature spell?

O let me, when Thy roof my soul hath hid,
   O let me roost and nestle there:
   Then of a sinner Thou art rid,
      And I of hope and fear.

Yet take Thy way; for sure Thy way is best:
   Stretch or contract me Thy poor debtor:
   This is but tuning of my breast,
      To make the music better.

Whether I fly with angels, fall with dust,
   Thy hands made both, and I am there.
   Thy power and love, my love and trust,
      Make one place everywhere.

THE TEMPER

IT cannot be. Where is that mighty joy,
   Which just now took up all my heart?
   Lord! if Thou must needs use Thy dart,
Save that, and me; or sin for both destroy.

The grosser world stands to Thy word and art;
  But Thy diviner world of grace
  Thou suddenly dost raise and race,
And every day a new Creator art.

O fix Thy chair of grace, that all my powers
  May also fix their reverence:
  For when Thou dost depart from hence,
They grow unruly, and sit in Thy bowers.

Scatter, or bind them all to bend to Thee:
  Though elements change, and heaven move;
  Let not Thy higher court remove,
But keep a standing Majesty in me.

JORDAN ✓ .

WHO says that fictions only and false hair
  Become a verse? Is there in truth no beauty?
Is all good structure in a winding stair?
May no lines pass, except they do their duty
  Not to a true, but painted chair?

Is it no verse, except enchanted groves
And sudden arbours shadow coarse-spun lines?
Must purling streams refresh a lover's loves?
Must all be veiled, while he that reads, divines,
  Catching the sense at two removes?

Shepherds are honest people; let them sing:
Riddle who list, for me, and pull for Prime:
I envy no man's nightingale or spring;
Nor let them punish me with loss of rhyme,
  Who plainly say, " My God, my King."

EMPLOYMENT

IF as a flower doth spread and die,
 Thou wouldst extend me to some good,
Before I were by frost's extremity
   Nipt in the bud;

The sweetness and the praise were Thine;
 But the extension and the room,
Which in Thy garland I should fill, were mine
   At Thy great doom.

For as Thou dost impart Thy grace,
 The greater shall our glory be.
The measure of our joys is in this place,
   The stuff with Thee.

Let me not languish then, and spend
 A life as barren to Thy praise
As is the dust, to which that life doth tend,
   But with delays.

All things are busy; only I
 Neither bring honey with the bees,
Nor flowers to make that, nor the husbandry
   To water these.

I am no link of Thy great chain,
 But all my company is a weed.
Lord, place me in Thy concert; give one strain
   To my poor need.

THE HOLY SCRIPTURES

PART I.

O BOOK! infinite sweetness! let my heart
  Suck every letter, and a honey gain,
    Precious for any grief in any part;
To clear the breast, to mollify all pain.

Thou art all health, health thriving, till it make
  A full eternity: thou art a mass
Of strange delights, where we may wish and take.
Ladies, look here; this is the thankful glass,

That mends the looker's eyes: this is the well
  That washes what it shows.   Who can endear
  Thy praise too much? thou art Heaven's lieger here,
Working against the states of death and hell.

  Thou art joy's handsel: heaven lies flat in thee,
  Subject to every mounter's bended knee.

PART II.

O THAT I knew how all thy lights combine,
  And the configurations of their glory!
    Seeing not only how each verse doth shine,
But all the constellations of the story.

This verse marks that, and both do make a motion
  Unto a third, that ten leaves off doth lie:
  Then as dispersed herbs do watch a potion,
These three make up some Christian's destiny.

Such are thy secrets, which my life makes good,
  And comments on thee: for in everything
Thy words do find me out, and parallels bring,
And in another make me understood.

  Stars are poor books, and oftentimes do miss:
 This book of stars lights to eternal bliss.

WHITSUNDAY

L ISTEN, sweet Dove, unto my song,
    And spread Thy golden wings in me;
  Hatching my tender heart so long,
Till it get wing, and fly away with Thee.

  Where is that fire which once descended
  On Thy Apostles? Thou didst then
  Keep open house, richly attended,
Feasting all comers by twelve chosen men.

  Such glorious gifts Thou didst bestow,
  That the earth did like a heaven appear:
  The stars were coming down to know
If they might mend their wages, and serve here.

  The sun, which once did shine alone,
  Hung down his head, and wished for night,
  When he beheld twelve suns for one
Going about the world, and giving light.

  But since those pipes of gold, which brought
  That cordial water to our ground,
  Were cut and martyred by the fault
Of those who did themselves through their side wound;

Thou shutt'st the door, and keep'st within ;
Scarce a good joy creeps through the chink ;
And if the braves of conquering sin
Did not excite Thee, we should wholly sink.

Lord, though we change, Thou art the same ;
The same sweet God of love and light :
Restore this day, for Thy great Name,
Unto his ancient and miraculous right.

GRACE

MY stock lies dead, and no increase
Doth my dull husbandry improve :
O let Thy graces without cease
          Drop from above!

If still the sun should hide his face,
Thy house would but a dungeon prove,
Thy works night's captives : O let grace
          Drop from above!

The dew doth every morning fall ;
And shall the dew outstrip Thy Dove?
The dew, for which grass cannot call,
          Drop from above.

Death is still working like a mole,
And digs my grave at each remove :
Let grace work too, and on my soul
          Drop from above.

Sin is still hammering my heart
Unto a hardness, void of love:
Let suppling grace, to cross his art,
          Drop from above.

O come! for Thou dost know the way.
Or if to me Thou wilt not move,
Remove me where I need not say—
         , Drop from above.

PRAISE

TO write a verse or two, is all the praise,
      That I can raise:
   Mend my estate in any ways,
    Thou shalt have more.

I go to Church; help me to wings, and I
      Will thither fly;
   Or, if I mount unto the sky,
    I will do more.

Man is all weakness; there is no such thing
      As prince or king:
   His arm is short; yet with a sling
    He may do more.

A herb distilled, and drunk,.may dwell next door,
      On the same floor,
   To a brave soul: exalt the poor,
    They can do more.

O raise me then ! poor bees, that work all day,
       Sting my delay,
    Who have a work, as well as they,
       And much, much more.

AFFLICTION

KILL me not every day,
    Thou Lord of life ! since Thy one death for me
    Is more than all my deaths can be,
       Though I in broken pay
Die over each hour of Methusalem's stay.

       If all men's tears were let
Into one common sewer, sea, and brine ;
    What were they all, compared to Thine ?
       Wherein if they were set,
They would discolour Thy most bloody sweat.

       Thou art my grief alone,
Thou Lord conceal it not : and as Thou art
    All my delight, so all my smart :
       Thy cross took up in one,
By way of imprest, all my future moan.

MATTINS

I CANNOT ope mine eyes,
    But Thou art ready there to catch
    My morning-soul and sacrifice :
Then we must needs for that day make a match.

My God, what is a heart?
Silver, or gold, or precious stone,
Or star, or rainbow, or a part
Of all these things, or all of them in one?

My God, what is a heart,
That Thou shouldst it so eye, and woo,
Pouring upon it all Thy art,
As if that Thou hadst nothing else to do?

Indeed, man's whole estate
Amounts (and richly) to serve Thee:
He did not heaven and earth create,
Yet studies them, not Him by whom they be.

Teach me Thy love to know;
That this new light, which now I see,
May both the work and workman show:
Then by a sunbeam I will climb to Thee.

SIN

O THAT I could a sin once see!
   We paint the devil foul, yet he
   Hath some good in him, all agree.
Sin is flat opposite to the Almighty, seeing
It wants the good of virtue, and of being.

But God more care of us hath had,
   If apparitions make us sad,
   By sight of sin we should grow mad.
Yet as in sleep we see foul death, and live;
So devils are our sins in prospective.

EVEN-SONG

BLEST be the God of love,
 Who gave me eyes, and light, and power this day,
 Both to be busy, and to play.
But much more blest be God above,

Who gave me sight alone,
Which to Himself He did deny:
For when He sees my ways, I die:
But I have got His Son, and He hath none.

What have I brought Thee home
For this Thy love? have I discharged the debt,
Which this day's favour did beget?
I ran; but all I brought was foam.

Thy diet, care, and cost
Do end in bubbles, balls of wind;
Of wind to Thee whom I have crost,
But balls of wild fire to my troubled mind.

Yet still Thou goest on,
And now with darkness closest weary eyes,
Saying to man, " It doth suffice:
Henceforth repose ; your work is done."

Thus in Thy ebony-box
Thou dost inclose us, till the day
Put our amendment in our way,
And give new wheels to our disordered clocks.

I muse, which shows more love,
The day or night? That is the gale, this the harbour;
That is the walk, and this the arbour;
Or that the garden, this the grove.

My God, Thou art all love.
Not one poor minute 'scapes thy breast,
But brings a favour from above;
And in this love, more than in bed, I rest.

CHURCH MONUMENTS

WHILE that my soul repairs to her devotion,
    Here I intomb my flesh, that it betimes
May take acquaintance of this heap of dust;
To which the blast of death's incessant motion,
Fed with the exhalation of our crimes,
Drives all at last.   Therefore I gladly trust

My body to this school, that it may learn
To spell his elements, and find his birth
Written in dusty heraldry and lines;
Which dissolution sure doth best discern,
Comparing dust with dust, and earth with earth.
These laugh at jet, and marble put for signs,

To sever the good fellowship of dust,
And spoil the meeting.   What shall point out them,
When they shall bow, and kneel, and fall down flat
To kiss those heaps, which now they have in trust?
Dear flesh, while I do pray, learn here thy stem
And true descent; that when thou shalt grow fat,

And wanton in thy cravings, thou mayst know,
That flesh is but the glass, which holds the dust
That measures all our time; which also shall
Be crumbled into dust. Mark, here below,
How tame these ashes are, how free from lust,
That thou mayst fit thyself against thy fall.

CHURCH MUSIC

SWEETEST of sweets, I thank you: when dis-
      pleasure
   Did through my body wound my mind.
You took me thence; and in your house of pleasure
   A dainty lodging me assigned.

Now I in you without a body move,
   Rising and falling with your wings:
We both together sweetly live and love,
   Yet say sometimes, " God help poor kings."

Comfort, I'll die; for if you post from me,
   Sure I shall do so, and much more:
But if I travel in your company,
   You know the way to heaven's door.

CHURCH LOCK AND KEY

I KNOW it is my sin, which locks Thine ears,
      And binds Thy hands!
Out-crying my requests, drowning my tears;
Or else the chillness of my faint demands.

But as cold hands are angry with the fire,
         And mend it still ;
So I do lay the want of my desire,
Not on my sins, or coldness, but Thy will.

Yet hear, O God, only for His blood's sake,
         Which pleads for me :
For though sins plead too, yet like stones they make
His blood's sweet current much more loud to be.

THE CHURCH-FLOOR

MARK you the floor? that square and speckled stone,
         Which looks so firm and strong,
                 Is Patience :

And the other black and grave, wherewith each one
         Is checker'd all along,
                 Humility :

The gentle rising, which on either hand
         Leads to the quire above,
                 Is Confidence :

But the sweet cement, which in one sure band
         Ties the whole frame, is Love
                 And Charity.

Hither sometimes Sin steals, and stains
The marble's neat and curious veins :

But all is cleansed when the marble weeps.
    Sometimes Death, puffing at the door,
    Blows all the dust about the floor :
But while he thinks to spoil the room, he sweeps.
    Blest be the Architect, whose art
    Could build so strong in a weak heart.

THE WINDOWS

LORD, how can man preach Thy eternal word?
    He is a brittle crazy glass :
Yet in Thy temple Thou dost him afford
    This glorious and transcendent place,
    To be a window, through Thy grace.

But when Thou dost anneal in glass Thy story,
    Making Thy life to shine within
The holy preachers, then the light and glory
    More reverend grows, and more doth win ;
    Which else shows waterish, bleak, and thin.

Doctrine and life, colours and light, in one
    When they combine and mingle, bring
A strong regard and awe : but speech alone
    Doth vanish like a flaring thing,
    And in the ear, not conscience ring.

TRINITY-SUNDAY

LORD, Who hast formed me out of mud,
    And hast redeemed me through Thy blood,
And sanctified me to do good ;

Purge all my sins done heretofore;
 For I confess my heavy score,
 And I will strive to sin no more.

Enrich my heart, mouth, hands in me,
 With faith, with hope, with charity;
 That I may run, rise, rest with Thee.

CONTENT

PEACE, muttering thoughts, and do not grudge
  to keep
 Within the walls of your own breast:
Who cannot on his own bed sweetly sleep,
 Can on another's hardly rest.

Gad not abroad at every quest and call
 Of an untrainèd hope or passion:
To court each place or fortune that doth fall,
 Is wantonness in contemplation.

Mark how the fire in flints doth quiet lie,
 Content and warm to itself alone:
But when it would appear to other's eye,
 Without a knock it never shone.

Give me the pliant mind, whose gentle measure
 Complies and suits with all estates;
Which can let loose to a crown, and yet with pleasure
 Take up within a cloister's gates.

This soul doth span the world, and hang content
 From either pole unto the centre:
Where in each room of the well-furnished tent
 He lies warm, and without adventure.

The brags of life are but a nine days' wonder :
    And after death the fumes that spring
From private bodies, make as big a thunder
    As those which rise from a huge king.

Only thy chronicle is lost : and yet
    Better by worms be all once spent,
Than to have hellish moths still gnaw and fret
    Thy name in books, which may not rent.

When all thy deeds, whose brunt thou feel'st alone,
    Are chawed by others' pens and tongues,
And as their wit is, their digestion,
    Thy nourished fame is weak or strong.

Then cease discoursing, soul ; till thine own ground ;
    Do not thyself or friends importune.
He that by seeking hath himself once found,
    Hath ever found a happy fortune.

THE QUIDDITY ✓

MY God a verse is not a crown ;
    No point of honour, or gay suit,
No hawk, or banquet, or renown,
    Nor a good sword, nor yet a lute :

It cannot vault, or dance, or play ;
It never was in France or Spain ;
Nor can it entertain the day
With a great stable or domain.

It is no office, art, or news ;
Nor the exchange or busy hall :
But it is that, which while I use,
I am with Thee, and "most take all."

HUMILITY

I SAW the Virtues sitting hand in hand
   In several ranks upon an azure throne,
Where all the beasts and fowls, by their command,
Presented tokens of submission.
Humility, who sat the lowest there
            To execute their call,
When by the beasts the presents tendered were,
            Gave them about to all.

The angry lion did present his paw,
Which by consent was given to mansuetude.
The fearful hare her ears, which by their law
Humility did reach to fortitude.
The jealous turkey brought his coral chain,
            That went to temperance.
On justice was bestowed the fox's brain,
            Killed in the way by chance.

At length the crow, bringing the peacock's plume,
(For he would not) as they beheld the grace
Of that brave gift, each one began to fume,
And challenge it, as proper to his place,
Till they fell out ; which when the beasts espied,
            They leapt upon the throne ;
And if the fox had lived to rule their side,
            They had deposed each one.

Humility, who held the plume, at this
Did weep so fast, that the tears trickling down
Spoiled all the train : then saying, " Here it is
For which ye wrangle," made them turn their frown
Against the beasts : so jointly bandying,
        They drive them soon away ;
And then amerced them, double gifts to bring
        At the next session-day.

FRAILTY

L ORD, in my silence how do I despise
        What upon trust
Is styled, honour, riches, or fair eyes ;
        But is—fair dust !
   I surname them gilded clay,
   Dear earth, fine grass or hay ;
In all, I think my foot doth ever tread
        Upon their head.

But when I view abroad both regiments,
        The world's, and Thine ;
Thine clad with simpleness, and sad events ;
        The other fine,
   Full of glory and gay weeds,
   Brave language, braver deeds :
That which was dust before, doth quickly rise,
        And prick mine eyes.

O brook not this, lest if what even now
        My foot doth tread,
Affront those joys, wherewith Thou didst endow,
        And long since wed

My poor soul, e'en sick of love ;
It may a Babel prove,
Commodious to conquer heaven and Thee
Planted in me.

CONSTANCY

WHO is the honest man?
     He that doth still and strongly good pursue,
To God, his neighbour, and himself most true :
     Whom neither force nor fawning can
Unpin, or wrench from giving all their due.

     Whose honesty is not
So loose or easy, that a ruffling wind
Can blow away, or glittering look it blind :
     Who rides his sure and even trot,
While the world now rides by, now lags behind.

     Who, when great trials come,
Nor seeks, nor shuns them ; but doth calmly stay,
Till he the thing and the example weigh :
     All being brought into a sum,
What place or person calls for, he doth pay.

     Whom none can work or woo,
To use in anything a trick or sleight ;
For above all things he abhors deceit :
     His words and works and fashion too
All of a piece, and all are clear and straight.

Who never melts or thaws
At close temptations : when the day is done,
His goodness sets not, but in dark can run :
  The sun to others writeth laws,
And is their virtue ; virtue is his sun.

  Who, when he is to treat
With sick folks, women, those whom passions sway,
Allows for that, and keeps his constant way :
  Whom others' faults do not defeat ;
But though men fail him, yet his part doth play.

  Whom nothing can procure,
When the wide world runs bias, from his will
To writhe his limbs, and share, not mend the ill.
  This is the marksman safe and sure,
Who still is right, and prays to be so still.

AFFLICTION ✓

M Y heart did heave, and there came forth, O God !
 By that I knew that Thou wast in the grief,
To guide and govern it to my relief,
  Making a sceptre of the rod :
  Hadst Thou not had Thy part,
Sure the unruly sigh had broke my heart.

But since Thy breath gave me both life and shape,
Thou know'st my tallies ; and when there's assigned
So much breath to a sigh, what's then behind?
  Or if some years with it escape,
  The sigh then only is
A gale to bring me sooner to my bliss.

Thy life on earth was grief, and Thou art still
Constant unto it, making it to be
A point of honour, now to grieve in me,
   And in Thy members suffer ill.
    They who lament one cross,
Thou dying daily, praise Thee to Thy loss.

THE STAR

BRIGHT spark, shot from a brighter place,
 Where beams surround my Saviour's face,
  Canst thou be anywhere
  So well as there?

Yet, if thou wilt from thence depart,
 Take a bad lodging in my heart;
  For thou canst make a debtor,
  And make it better.

First with thy fire-work burn to dust
 Folly, and worse than folly, lust:
  Then with thy light refine,
  And make it shine.

So disengaged from sin and sickness,
 Touch it with thy celestial quickness,
  That it may hang and move
  After thy love.

Then with our trinity of light,
 Motion, and heat; let's take our flight
  Unto the place where thou
  Before didst bow.

Get me a standing there, and place
  Among the beams, which crown the face,
    Of Him, who died to part
      Sin and my heart:

That so among the rest I may
  Glitter, and curl, and wind as they:
    That winding is their fashion
      Of adoration.

Sure thou wilt joy by gaining me
  To fly home like a laden bee
    Unto that hive of beams
      And garland-streams.

SUNDAY

O DAY mos. calm, most bright,
  The fruit of this, the next world's bud,
The indorsement of supreme delight,
Writ by a Friend, and with His blood;
The couch of time; care's balm and bay;
The week were dark, but for thy light:
    Thy torch doth show the way.

    The other days and thou
Make up one man; whose face thou art,
Knocking at heaven with thy brow:
The worky-days are the back-part;
The burden of the week lies there,
Making the whole to stoop and bow,
    Till thy release appear.

Man had straight forward gone
To endless death; but thou dost pull
And turn us round to look on One,
Whom, if we were not very dull,
We could not choose but look on still;
Since there is no place so alone
     The which He doth not fill.

Sundays the pillars are,
On which heaven's palâce archèd lies:
The other days fill up the spare
And hollow room with vanities.
They are the fruitful beds and borders
In God's rich garden: that is bare
     Which parts their ranks and orders.

The Sundays of man's life,
Threaded together on time's string,
Make bracelets to adorn the wife
Of the eternal glorious King.
On Sunday heaven's gate stands ope;
Blessings are plentiful and rife,
     More plentiful than hope.[1]

This day my Saviour rose,
And did enclose this light for His:
That, as each beast his manger knows,
Man might not of his fodder miss.
Christ hath took in this piece of ground,
And made a garden there for those
     Who want herbs for their wound.

The rest of our creation
Our great Redeemer did remove

1 [Herbert sang this stanza to the accompaniment of his lute the
Sunday before his death.]

With the same shake, which at His passion
Did the earth and all things with it move.
As Samson bore the doors away,
Christ's hands, though nailed, wrought our salvation,
    And did unhinge that day.

    The brightness of that day
We sullied by our foul offence:
Wherefore that robe we cast away,
Having a new at His expense,
Whose drops of blood paid the full price,
That was required to make us gay,
    And fit for Paradise.

    Thou art a day of mirth:
And where the week days trail on ground,
Thy flight is higher, as thy birth:
O let me take thee at the bound,
Leaping with thee from seven to seven,
Till that we both, being tossed from earth,
    Fly hand in hand to heaven!

AVARICE

MONEY, thou bane of bliss, and source of woe,
    Whence comest thou, that thou art so fresh
        and fine?
    I know thy parentage is base and low:
Man found thee poor and dirty in a mine.

Sure thou didst so little contribute
    To this great kingdom, which thou now hast got,
    That he was fain, when thou wast destitute,
To dig thee out of thy dark cave and grot.

Then forcing thee, by fire he made thee bright :
   Nay, thou hast got the face of man ; for we
   Have with our stamp and seal transferred our right :
Thou art the man, and man but dross to thee.

Man calleth thee his wealth, who made thee rich ;
And while he digs out thee, falls in the ditch.

ANA- { MARY / ARMY } GRAM

H OW well her name an ARMY doth present,
   In whom the LORD OF HOSTS did pitch His tent !

TO ALL ANGELS AND SAINTS

O GLORIOUS spirits, who after all your bands
   See the smooth face of God, without a frown,
         Or strict commands ;
Where every one is king, and hath his crown,
If not upon his head, yet in his hands :

Not out of envy or maliciousness
Do I forbear to crave your special aid.
         I would address
My vows to thee most gladly, blessed Maid,
And Mother of my God, in my distress :

Thou art the holy mine, whence came the gold,
The great restorative for all decay
         In young and old ;

Thou art the cabinet where the jewel lay:
Chiefly to thee would I my soul unfold.

But now, alas! I dare not; for our King,
Whom we do all jointly adore and praise,
    Bids no such thing:
And where His pleasure no injunction lays,
('Tis your own case) ye never move a wing.

All worship is prerogative, and a flower
Of His rich crown, from whom lies no appeal
    At the last hour:
Therefore we dare not from His garland steal,
To make a posy for inferior power.

Although then others court you, if ye know
What's done on earth, we shall not fare the worse,
    Who do not so;
Since we are ever ready to disburse,
If any one our Master's hand can show.

EMPLOYMENT

HE that is weary, let him sit.
    My soul would stir
And trade in courtesies and wit,
    Quitting the fur,
To cold complexions needing it.

Man is no star, but a quick coal
    Of mortal fire:
Who blows it not, nor doth control
    A faint desire,
Lets his own ashes choke his soul.

When the elements did for place contest
        With Him, whose will
Ordained the highest to be best :
        The earth sat still,
And by the others is opprest.

Life is a business, not good cheer ;
        Ever in wars.
The sun still shineth there or here,
        Whereas the stars
Watch an advantage to appear.

O that I were an orange-tree,
        That busy plant!
Then should I ever laden be,
        And never want
Some fruit for Him that dresseth me.

But we are still too young or old ;
        The man is gone,
Before we do our wares unfold :
        So we freeze on,
Until the grave increase our cold.

DENIAL

WHEN my devotions could not pierce
        Thy silent ears ;
Then was my heart broken, as was my verse ;
        My breast was full of fears
           And disorder.

My bent thoughts, like a brittle bow,
  Did fly asunder:
Each took his way; some would to pleasures go,
  Some to the wars and thunder
    Of alarms.

As good go anywhere they say,
  As to benumb
Both knees and heart, in crying night and day.
  "Come, come, my God, O come!"
    But no hearing.

O, that Thou shouldst give dust a tongue
  To cry to Thee,
And then not hear it crying! all day long
  My heart was in my knee,
    But no hearing.

Therefore my soul lay out of sight,
  Untuned, unstrung:
My feeble spirit, unable to look right,
  Like a nipt blossom, hung
    Discontented.

O cheer and tune my heartless breast,
  Defer no time;
That so Thy favours granting my request,
  They and my mind may chime,
    And mend my rhyme.

CHRISTMAS

ALL after pleasures as I rid one day,
   My horse and I, both tired, body and mind,
   With full cry of affections, quite astray;
I took up in the next inn I could find.

There, when I came, whom found I but my dear,
   My dearest Lord, expecting till the grief
   Of pleasures brought me to him, ready there
To be all passengers' most sweet relief?

O Thou, whose glorious, yet contracted light,
   Wrapt in night's mantle, stole into a manger;
   Since my dark soul and brutish is Thy right,
To man of all beasts be not Thou a stranger.

   Furnish and deck my soul, that Thou mayst have
   A better lodging than a rack or grave.

THE shepherds sing; and shall I silent be?
    My God, no hymn for Thee?
My soul's a shepherd too: a flock it feeds
    Of thoughts, and words, and deeds.
The pasture is Thy word; the streams, Thy grace
    Enriching all the place.
Shepherd and flock shall sing, and all my powers
    Out-sing the daylight hours.
Then we will chide the sun for letting night
    Take up his place and right:
We sing one common Lord; wherefore he should
    Himself the candle hold.

I will go searching, till I find a sun
     Shall stay, till we have done;
A willing shiner, that shall shine as gladly,
     As frost-nipt suns look sadly.
Then we will sing, and shine all our own day,
     And one another pay: •
His beams shall cheer my breast, and both so twine,
Till even his beams sing, and my music shine.

UNGRATEFULNESS

L ORD, with what bounty and rare clemency
     Hast Thou redeemed us from the grave!
     If Thou hadst let us run,
Gladly had man adored the sun,
     And thought his god most brave;
Where now we shall be better gods than he.

Thou hast but two rare cabinets full of treasure,
     The Trinity and Incarnation:
     Thou hast unlocked them both,
And made them jewels to betroth
     The work of Thy creation
Unto Thyself in everlasting pleasure.

The statelier cabinet is the Trinity,
     Whose sparkling light access denies:
     Therefore Thou dost not show
This fully to us, till death blow
     The dust into our eyes;
For by that powder thou wilt make us see.

But all Thy sweets are packed up in the other;
     Thy mercies thither flock and flow;

That, as the first affrights,
This may allure us with delights;
Because this box we know;
For we have all of us just such another.

But man is close, reserved, and dark to Thee;
When Thou demandest but a heart,
He cavils instantly.
In his poor cabinet of bone
Sins have their box apart,
Defrauding Thee, who gavest two for one.

SIGHS AND GROANS

O DO not use me
After my sins! look not on my desert,
But on Thy glory! then Thou wilt reform,
And not refuse me: for Thou only art
The mighty God, but I a silly worm:
O do not bruise me!

O do not urge me!
For what account can Thy ill steward make?
I have abused Thy stock, destroyed Thy woods,
Sucked all Thy magazines: my head did ache,
Till it found out how to consume Thy goods:
O do not scourge me!

O do not blind me!
I have deserved that an Egyptian night
Should thicken all my powers; because my lust
Hath still sew'd fig-leaves to exclude Thy light:
But I am frailty, and already dust:.
O do not grind me!

O do not fill me
With the turned vial of Thy bittter wrath!
For Thou hast other vessels full of blood,
A part whereof my Saviour emptied hath,
Even unto death : since He died for my good,
  O do not kill me!

But O, reprieve me!
For Thou hast life and death at Thy command;
Thou art both Judge and Saviour, feast and rod,
Cordial and corrosive : put not Thy hand
Into the bitter box ; but O my God,
  My God, relieve me.

THE WORLD

LOVE built a stately house ; where Fortune came;
 And spinning fancies she was heard to say,
That her fine cobwebs did support the frame,
Whereas they were supported by the same ·
But Wisdom quickly swept them all away.

Then Pleasure came, who, liking not the fashion,
Began to make balconies, terraces,
Till she had weakened all by alteration :
But reverend laws, and many a proclamation
Reformed all at length with menaces.

Then entered Sin, and with that sycamore,
Whose leaves first sheltered man from drought and
Working and winding slily evermore, [dew,
The inward walls and summers cleft and tore :
But Grace shored these, and cut that as it grew.

Then Sin combined with Death in a firm band,
To raze the building to the very floor:
Which they effected, none could them withstand;
But Love and Grace took Glory by the hand,
And built a braver palace than before.

OUR LIFE IS HID WITH CHRIST IN GOD

COLOSSIANS iii. 3.

$M$$Y$ words and thoughts do both express this
notion,
That *LIFE* hath with the sun a double motion.
The first *IS* straight, and our diurnal friend;
The other *HID*, and doth obliquely bend.
One life is wrapt *IN* flesh, and tends to earth:
The other winds towards *HIM*, whose happy birth
Taught me to live here so, *THAT* still one eye
Should aim and shoot at that which *IS* on high;
Quitting with daily labour all *MY* pleasure,
To gain at harvest an eternal *TREASURE*.

VANITY

THE fleet astronomer can bore   [mind:
    And thread the spheres with his quick-piercing
He views their stations, walks from door to door,
        Surveys, as if he had designed
To make a purchase there: he sees their dances,
            And knoweth long before,
Both their full-eyed aspects, and secret glances.

The nimble diver with his side
Cuts through the working waves, that he may fetch
His dearly-earned pearl, which God did hide
    On purpose from the venturous wretch;
That He might save his life, and also hers,
    Who with excessive pride
Her own destruction and his danger wears.

The subtile chymic can divest
And strip the creature naked, till he find
    The callow principles within their nest:
    There he imparts to them his mind,
Admitted to their bed-chamber, before
    They appear trim and drest
To ordinary suitors at the door.

What hath not man sought out and found,
But his dear God? who yet His glorious law
    Embosoms in us, mellowing the ground
    With showers and frosts, with love and awe;
So that we need not say, where's this command?
    Poor man! thou searchest round
-To find out death, but missest life at hand.

LENT

WELCOME, dear feast of Lent: who loves not
  He loves not temperance, or authority,   [thee,
    But is composed of passion.
The Scriptures bid us fast; the Church says, now:
Give to my mother what thou wouldst allow
    To every corporation.

The humble soul, composed of love and fear,
Begins at home, and lays the burden there,
       When doctrines disagree:
He says, in things which use hath justly got,
' I am a scandal to the Church,' and not
       ' The Church is so to me.'

True Christians should be glad of an occasion
To use their temperance, seeking no evasion,
       When good is seasonable;
Unless authority, which should increase
The obligation in us, make it less,
       And power itself disable.

Besides the cleanness of sweet abstinence,
Quick thoughts and motions at a small expense,
       A face not fearing light:
Whereas in fulness there are sluttish fumes,
Sour exhalations, and dishonest rheums,
       Revenging the delight.

Then those same pendent profits, which the spring
And Easter intimate, enlarge the thing,
       And goodness of the deed.
Neither ought other men's abuse of Lent
Spoil the good use; lest by that argument
       We forfeit all our creed.

'Tis true, we cannot reach Christ's fortieth day;
Yet to go part of that religious way
       Is better than to rest:
We cannot reach our Saviour's purity;
Yet are we bid, " Be holy e'en as He."
       In both let's do our best.

Who goeth in the way which Christ hath gone,
Is much more sure to meet with Him, than one
    That travelleth by-ways.
Perhaps my God, though He be far before,
May turn, and take me by the hand, and more,
    May strengthen my decays.

Yet, Lord, instruct us to improve our fast
By starving sin, and taking such repast
    As may our faults control:
That every man may revel at his door,
Not in his parlour; banqueting the poor,
    And among those his soul.

VIRTUE

SWEET day, so cool, so calm, so bright,
    The bridal of the earth and sky,
The dew shall weep thy fall to-night;
        For thou must die.

Sweet rose, whose hue angry and brave
Bids the rash gazer wipe his eye,
Thy root is ever in its grave,
        And thou must die.

Sweet spring, full of sweet days and roses,
A box where sweets compacted lie,
My music shows ye have your closes,
        And all must die.

Only a sweet and virtuous soul,
Like seasoned timber, never gives;
But though the whole world turn to coal,
        Then chiefly lives.

THE PEARL

MATT. xiii. 46.

I KNOW the ways of learning; both the head
   And pipes that feed the press, and make it run;
What reason hath from nature borrowed,
Or of itself, like a good housewife, spun
In laws and policy; what the stars conspire,
What willing nature speaks, what forced by fire;
Both the old discoveries, and the new-found seas,
The stock and surplus, cause and history:
All these stand open, or I have the keys:
        Yet I love Thee.

I know the ways of honour, what maintains
The quick returns of courtesy and wit:
In vies of favours whether party gains,
When glory swells the heart, and mouldeth it
To all expressions both of hand and eye,
Which on the world a true-love knot may tie,
And bear the bundle, wheresoe'er it goes:
How many drams of spirit there must be
To sell my life unto my friends or foes:
        Yet I love Thee.

I know the ways of pleasure, the sweet strains,
The lullings and the relishes of it;
The propositions of hot blood and brains;
What mirth and music mean; what love and wit

Have done these twenty hundred years, and more :
I know the projects of unbridled store :
My stuff is flesh, not brass; my senses live,
And grumble oft, that they have more in me
Than he that curbs them, being but one to five :
        Yet I love Thee.

I know all these, and have them in my hand :
Therefore not sealed, but with open eyes
I fly to Thee, and fully understand
Both the main sale, and the commodities;
And at what rate and price I have Thy love;
With all the circumstances that may move :
Yet through the labyrinths, not my grovelling wit,
But Thy silk-twist let down from heaven to me,
Did both conduct and teach me, how by it
        To climb to Thee.

AFFLICTION

BROKEN in pieces all asunder,
      Lord, hunt me not,
      A thing forgot,
Once a poor creature, now a wonder,
    A wonder tortured in the space
    Betwixt this world and that of grace.

My thoughts are all a case of knives,
      Wounding my heart
      With scattered smart ;
As watering-pots give flowers their lives.
    Nothing their fury can control,
    While they do wound and prick my soul.

All my attendants are at strife,
    Quitting their place
    Unto my face:
Nothing performs the task of life:
  The elements are let loose to fight,
  And while I live, try out their right.

O help, my God! let not their plot
    Kill them and me,
    And also Thee,
Who art my life: dissolve the knot,
  As the sun scatters by his light
  All the rebellions of the night.

Then shall those powers, which work for grief,
    Enter Thy pay,
    And day by day
Labour Thy praise and my relief:
  With care and courage building me,
  Till I reach heaven, and much more, Thee.

MAN

MY God, I heard this day,
  That none doth build a stately habitation,
   But he that means to dwell therein.
   What house more stately hath there been,
Or can be, than is Man? to whose creation
   All things are in decay.

  For Man is everything,
And more: he is a tree, yet bears no fruit;

A beast, yet is, or should be more:
Reason and speech we only bring.
Parrots may thank us, if they are not mute,
    They go upon the score.

    Man is all symmetry,
Full of proportions, one limb to another,
    And all to all the world besides:
    Each part may call the farthest, brother:
For head with foot hath private amity,
    And both with moons and tides.

    Nothing hath got so far,
But Man hath caught and kept it, as his prey.
    His eyes dismount the highest star:
    He is in little all the sphere.
Herbs gladly cure our flesh, because that they
    Find their acquaintance there.

    For us the winds do blow;
The earth doth rest, heaven move, and fountains flow.
    Nothing we see but means our good,
    As our delight, or as our treasure:
The whole is, either our cupboard of food,
    Or cabinet of pleasure.

    The stars have us to bed;
Night draws the curtain, which the sun withdraws:
    Music and light attend our head.
    All things unto our flesh are kind
In their descent and being; to our mind
    In their ascent and cause.

    Each thing is full of duty:
Waters united are our navigation;

Distinguished, our habitation;
Below, our drink; above, our meat:
Both are our cleanliness.   Hath one such beauty?
     Then how are all things neat!

     More servants wait on Man,
Than he'll take notice of: in every path
    He treads down that which doth befriend him,
 - When sickness makes him pale and wan.
O mighty love! Man is one world, and hath
    Another to attend him.

     Since then, my God, Thou hast
So brave a palace built; O dwell in it,
    That it may dwell with Thee at last!
    Till then, afford us so much wit,
That, as the world serves us, we may serve Thee,
    And both Thy servants be.

ANTIPHON

Chor. PRAISED be the God of love,
       Men. Here below,
     Angels. And here above:
Chor. Who hath dealt His mercies so,
     Ang. To His friend,
     Men. And to His foe;

Chor. That both grace and glory tend
     Ang. Us of old,
     Men. And us in the end.

Chor. The great Shepherd of the fold
     Ang. Us did make,
     Men. For us was sold.

Chor. He our foes in pieces brake:
     Ang. Him we touch;
     Men. And Him we take.
Chor. Wherefore since that He is such,
     Ang. We adore,
     Men. And we do crouch.

Chor. Lord, Thy praises shall be more.
     Men. We have none,
     Ang. And we no store.
Chor. Praised be the God alone
     Who hath made of two folds one.

UNKINDNESS

LORD, make me coy and tender to offend:
   In friendship first, I think, if that agree,
       Which I intend,
   Unto my friend's intent and end.
I would not use a friend, as I use Thee.

If any touch my friend, or his good name,
It is my honour and my love to free
       His blasted fame
   From the least spot or thought of blame.
I could not use a friend, as I use Thee.

My friend may spit upon my curious floor:
Would he have gold? I lend it instantly;
               But let the poor,
    And Thou within them starve at door.
I cannot use a friend, as I use Thee.

When that my friend pretendeth to a place,
I quit my interest, and leave it free:
               But when Thy grace
    Sues for my heart, I Thee displace;
Nor would I use a friend, as I use Thee.

Yet can a friend what Thou hast done fulfil:
O write in brass, " My God upon a tree
               " His blood did spill,
    " Only to purchase my good will:
" Yet use I not my foes, as I use Thee."

LIFE

I MADE a posy, while the day ran by:
    Here will I smell my remnant out, and tie
               My life within this band.
But time did beckon to the flowers, and they
By noon most cunningly did steal away,
               And withered in my hand.

My hand was next to them, and then my heart;
I took, without more thinking, in good part
               Time's gentle admonition;
Who did so sweetly death's sad taste convey,
Making my mind to smell my fatal day,
               Yet sugaring the suspicion.

Farewell, dear flowers, sweetly your time ye spent,
Fit, while ye lived, for smell or ornament,
      And after death for cures.
I follow straight without complaints or grief,
Since if my scent be good, I care not if
      It be as short as yours.

SUBMISSION

BUT that Thou art my wisdom, Lord,
      And both mine eyes are Thine,
My mind would be extremely stirred
      For missing my design.

Were it not better to bestow
      Some place and power on me?
Then should Thy praises with me grow,
      And share in my degree.

But when I thus dispute and grieve,
      I do resume my sight;
And pilfering what I once did give,
      Disseize Thee of Thy right.

How know I, if Thou shouldst me raise,
      That I should then raise Thee?
Perhaps great places and Thy praise
      Do not so well agree.

Wherefore unto my gift I stand;
      I will no more advise:
Only do Thou lend me a hand,
      Since Thou hast both mine eyes.

JUSTICE

I CANNOT skill of these my ways
  "Lord, Thou didst make me, yet Thou woundest
    me:
"Lord, Thou dost wound me, yet Thou dost relieve
    me:
"Lord, Thou relievest, yet I die by Thee:
"Lord, Thou dost kill me, yet Thou dost reprieve me."

    But when I mark my life and praise,
      Thy justice me most fitly pays:
For "I do praise Thee, yet I praise Thee not:
"My prayers mean Thee, yet my prayers stray:
"I would do well, yet sin the hand hath got:
"My soul doth love Thee, yet it loves delay."
      I cannot skill of these my ways.

CHARMS AND KNOTS

WHO read a chapter when they rise,
  Shall ne'er be troubled with ill eyes.

A poor man's rod, when thou dost ride,
Is both a weapon and a guide.

Who shuts his hand, hath lost his gold;
Who opens it, hath it twice told.

Who goes to bed, and doth not pray,
Maketh two nights to every day.

Who by aspersions throw a stone
At the head of others, hit their own.

Who looks on ground with humble eyes,
Finds himself there, and seeks to rise.

When the hair is sweet through pride or lust,
The powder doth forget the dust.

Take one from ten, and what remains?
Ten still, if sermons go for gains.

In shallow waters heaven doth show:
But who drinks on, to hell may go.

AFFLICTION

MY God, I read this day,
    That planted Paradise was not so firm
As was and is Thy floating Ark; whose stay
And anchor Thou art only, to confirm
      And strengthen it in every age,
      When waves do rise, and tempests rage.

      At first we lived in pleasure;
Thine own delights Thou didst to us impart:
When we grew wanton, thou didst use displeasure
To make us Thine: yet that we might not part,
      As we at first did board with Thee,
      Now Thou wouldst taste our misery.

      There is but joy and grief;
If either will convert us, we are Thine:

Some Angels used the first; if our relief
Take up the second, then Thy double line
    And several baits in either kind
    Furnish Thy table to Thy mind.

    Affliction then is ours;
We are the trees, whom shaking fastens more,
While blustering winds destroy the wanton bowers,
And ruffle all their curious knots and store.
    My God, so temper joy and woe,
    That Thy bright beams may tame Thy bow.

MORTIFICATION

H OW soon doth man decay!
    When clothes are taken from a chest of sweets
    To swaddle infants, whose young breath
        Scarce knows the way;
Those clouts are little winding-sheets,
Which do consign and send them unto death.

    When boys go first to bed,
They step into their voluntary graves;
    Sleep binds them fast; only their breath
        Makes them not dead.
Successive nights, like rolling waves,
Convey them quickly, who are bound for death.

    When youth is frank and free,
And calls for music, while his veins do swell,
    All day exchanging mirth and breath
        In company;
That music summons to the knell,
Which shall befriend him at the house of death.

When man grows staid and wise,
Getting a house and home, where he may move
Within the circle of his breath,
Schooling his eyes;
That dumb inclosure maketh love
Unto the coffin, that attends his death.

When age grows low and weak,
Marking his grave, and thawing every year,
Till all do melt, and drown his breath
When he would speak;
A chair or litter shows the bier
Which shall convey him to the house of death.

Man, ere he is aware,
Hath put together a solemnity,
And drest his hearse, while he has breath
As yet to spare.
Yet, Lord, instruct us so to die
That all these dyings may be life in death.

DECAY

SWEET were the days, when Thou didst lodge
with Lot,
Struggle with Jacob, sit with Gideon,
Advise with Abraham, when Thy power could not
Encounter Moses' strong complaints and moan:
Thy words were then, " Let Me alone."

One might have sought and found Thee presently
At some fair oak, or bush, or cave, or well:

Is my God this way?   No, they would reply;
He is to Sinai gone, as we heard tell:
　　　List, ye may hear great Aaron's bell.

But now Thou dost Thyself immure and close
In some one corner of a feeble heart:
Where yet both sin and Satan, Thy old foes,
Do pinch and straiten Thee, and use much art
　　　To gain Thy thirds and little part.

I see the world grows old, when as the heat
Of Thy great love once spread, as in an urn
Doth closet up itself, and still retreat,
Cold sin still forcing it, till it return
　　　And calling justice, all things burn.

MISERY

LORD, let the Angels praise Thy name.
　　Man is a foolish thing, a foolish thing;
　　Folly and sin play all his game.
His house still burns; and yet he still doth sing,
　　　" Man is but grass,
　　　" He knows it, fill the glass."

How canst Thou brook his foolishness?
Why, he'll not lose a cup of drink for Thee:
　　Bid him but temper his excess;
Not he: he knows where he can better be,
　　　As he will swear,
　　　Than to serve Thee in fear.

What strange pollutions doth he wed,
And make his own! as if none knew, but he.
No man shall beat into his head
That Thou within his curtains drawn canst see:
Were they of cloth,
Where never yet came moth.

The best of men, turn but Thy hand
For one poor minute, stumble at a pin:
They would not have their actions scanned,
Nor any sorrow tell them that they sin,
Though it be small,
And measure not their fall.

They quarrel Thee, and would give over
The bargain made to serve Thee: but Thy love
Holds them unto it, and doth cover
Their follies with the wing of Thy mild Dove,
Not suffering those
Who would, to be Thy foes.

My God, man cannot praise Thy name:
Thou art all brightness, perfect purity:
The sun holds down his head for shame,
Dead with eclipses, when we speak of Thee.
How shall infection
Presume on Thy perfection?

As dirty hands foul all they touch,
And those things most, which are most pure and fine:
So our clay-hearts, e'en when we crouch
To sing Thy praises, make them less divine.
Yet either this
Or none Thy portion is.

Man cannot serve Thee; let him go
And serve the swine: there, there is his delight:
He doth not like this virtue, no;
Give him his dirt to wallow in all night;
         These preachers make
        His head to shoot and ache.

O foolish man! where are thine eyes?
How hast Thou lost them in a crowd of cares?
Thou pullest the rug, and wilt not rise,
No, not to purchase the whole pack of stars:
         There let them shine,
        Thou must go sleep, or dine.

The bird that sees a dainty bower
Made in the tree, where she was wont to sit,
Wonders and sings, but not His power
Who made the arbour: this exceeds her wit.
         But man doth know
        The spring whence all things flow:

And yet as though he knew it not,
His knowledge winks, and lets his humours reign:
They make his life a constant blot,
And all the blood of God to run in vain.
         Ah, wretch! what verse
        Can thy strange ways rehearse?

Indeed at first man was a treasure,
A box of jewels, shop of rarities
A ring, whose posy was, " My pleasure:"
He was a garden in a Paradise:
         Glory and grace
        Did crown his heart and face.

But sin hath fooled him.   Now he is
A lump of flesh, without a foot or wing
To raise him to the glimpse of bliss:
A sick tossed vessel, dashing on each thing;
        Nay, his own shelf:
    My God, I mean myself.

JORDAN

WHEN first my lines of heavenly joys made
      mention,
Such was their lustre, they did so excel,
That I sought out quaint words, and trim invention;
My thoughts began to burnish, sprout, and swell,
Curling with metaphors a plain intention,
Decking the sense, as if it were to sell.

Thousands of notions in my brain did run,
Offering their service, if I were not sped:
I often blotted what I had begun;
This was not quick enough, and that was dead.
Nothing could seem too rich to clothe the sun,
Much less those joys which trample on his head.

As flames do work and wind, when they ascend;
So did I weave myself into the sense.
But while I bustled, I might hear a friend
Whisper, " How wide is all this long pretence!
" There is in love a sweetness ready penned:
" Copy out only that, and save expense."

PRAYER

OF what an easy, quick access,
  My blessed Lord, art Thou! how suddenly
    May our requests Thine ear invade!
To show that state dislikes not easiness.
If I but lift mine eyes, my suit is made:
Thou canst no more not hear, than Thou canst die.

Of what supreme Almighty power
Is Thy great arm which spans the east and west,
    And tacks the centre to the sphere!
By it do all things live their measured hour:
We cannot ask the thing, which is not there,
Blaming the shallowness of our request.

Of what unmeasurable love
Art Thou possest, who, when Thou couldst not die,
    Wert fain to take our flesh and curse,
And for our sakes in person sin reprove;
That by destroying that which tied Thy purse,
Thou mightst make way for liberality!

Since then these three wait on Thy throne,
Ease, Power, and Love; I value Prayer so,
    That were I to leave all but one,
Wealth, fame, endowments, virtues, all should go;
I and dear Prayer would together dwell,
And quickly gain, for each inch lost, an ell.

OBEDIENCE

MY God, if writings may
        Convey a lordship any way
Whither the buyer and the seller please;
        Let it not Thee displease,
If this poor paper do as much as they.

        On it my heart doth bleed
        As many lines, as there doth need
To pass itself and all it hath to Thee.
        To which I do agree,
And here present it as my special deed.

        If that hereafter pleasure
        Cavil, and claim her part and measure,
As if this passed with a reservation,
        Or some such words in fashion;
I here exclude the wrangler from Thy treasure.

        O let Thy sacred will
        All Thy delight in me fulfil!
Let me not think an action mine own way,
        But as Thy love shall sway,
Resigning up the rudder to Thy skill.

        Lord what is man to Thee,
        That Thou shouldst mind a rotten tree?
Yet since Thou canst not choose but see my actions?
        So great are Thy perfections,
Thou mayst as well my actions guide, as see.

        Besides, Thy death and blood
        Showed a strange love to all our good:

Thy sorrows were in earnest; no faint proffer,
    Or superficial offer
Of what we might not take, or be withstood.

    Wherefore I all forego:
To one word only I say, No:
Where in the deed there was an intimation
    Of a gift or donation,
Lord, let it now by way of purchase go.

    He that will pass his land,
As I have mine, may set his hand
And heart into this deed, when he hath read:
    And make the purchase spread
To both our goods, if he to it will stand.

    How happy were my part,
If some kind man would thrust his heart
Into these lines; till in heaven's court of rolls
    They were by winged souls
Entered for both, far above their desert!

CONSCIENCE

PEACE, prattler, do not lour:
    Not a fair look, but thou dost call it foul:
Not a sweet dish, but thou dost call it sour:
    Music to thee doth howl.
    By listening to thy chatting fears
    I have both lost mine eyes and ears.

Prattler, no more, I say:
My thoughts must work, but like a noiseless sphere.
Harmonious peace must rock them all the day:
 No room for prattlers there.
 If thou persisteth, I will tell thee,
 That I have physic to expel thee.

 And the receipt shall be
My Saviour's blood: whenever at His board
I do but taste it, straight it cleanseth me,
 And leaves thee not a word;
 No, not a tooth or nail to scratch,
 And at my actions carp, or catch.

 Yet if thou talkest still,
Besides my physic, know there's some for thee:
Some wood and nails to make a staff or bill
 For those that trouble me:
 The bloody cross of my dear Lord
 Is both my physic and my sword.

SION

LORD, with what glory wast Thou served of old,
 When Solomon's temple stood and flourished!
 Where most things were of purest gold;
 The wood was all embellished
With flowers and carvings, mystical and rare:
All showed the builders craved the seer's care.

Yet all this glory, all this pomp and state,
Did not affect Thee much, was not Thy aim,
 Something there was that sowed debate:
 Wherefore Thou quitt'st Thy ancient claim:

And now Thy architecture meets with sin:
For all Thy frame and fabric is within.

There Thou art struggling with a peevish heart,
Which sometimes crosseth Thee, Thou sometimes it:
   The fight is hard on either part.
   Great God doth fight, He doth submit.
All Solomon's sea of brass and world of stone
Is not so dear to Thee as one good groan.

And truly brass and stones are heavy things,
Tombs for the dead, not temples fit for Thee:
   But groans are quick, and full of wings,
   And all their motions upward be;
And ever as they mount, like larks they sing:
The note is sad, yet music for a King.

HOME

COME, Lord, my head doth burn, my heart is sick,
   While Thou dost ever, ever stay:
Thy long deferrings wound me to the quick,
   My spirit gaspeth night and day.
      O show Thyself to me,
      Or take me up to Thee!

How canst Thou stay, considering the pace
   The blood did make, which thou didst waste?
When I behold it trickling down thy face,
   I never saw thing make such haste.
      O show Thyself, &c.

When man was lost, Thy pity looked about,
   To see what help in the earth or sky :
But there was none ; at least no help without :
   The help did in Thy bosom lie.
        O show Thyself, &c.

There lay Thy Son : and must He leave that nest,
   That hive of sweetness, to remove
Thraldom for those, who would not at a feast
   Leave one poor apple for Thy love ?
        O show Thyself, &c.

He did, He came : O my Redeemer dear,
   After all this canst Thou be strange ?
So many years baptized, and not appear ;
   As if Thy love could fail or change ?
        O show Thyself, &c.

Yet if Thou stayest still, why must I stay ?
   My God, what is this world to me ?
This world of woe ? hence, all ye clouds, away,
   Away ; I must get up and see.
        O show Thyself, &c.

What is this weary world ; this meat and drink,
   That chains us by the teeth so fast ?
What is this woman-kind, which I can wink
   Into a blackness and distaste ?
        O show Thyself, &c.

With one small sigh Thou gavest me the other day
   I blasted all the joys about me :
And scowling on them as they pined away,
   Now come again, said I, and flout me.
        O show Thyself, &c.

Nothing but drought and dearth, but bush and brake,
     Which way soe'er I look, I see.
Some may dream merrily, but when they wake,
     They dress themselves and come to Thee.
          O show Thyself, &c.

We talk of harvests ; there are no such things,
     But when we leave our corn and hay :
There is no fruitful year, but that which brings
     The last and loved, though dreadful day.
          O show Thyself, &c.

O loose this frame, this knot of man untie,
     That my free soul may use her wing,
Which now is pinioned with mortality,
     As an entangled, hampered thing.
          O show Thyself, &c.

What have I left that I should stay and groan?
     The most of me to heaven is fled :
My thoughts and joys are all packed up and gone,
     And for their old acquaintance plead.
          O show Thyself, &c.

Come, dearest Lord, pass not this holy season,
     My flesh and bones and joints do pray :
And e'en my verse, when by the rhyme and reason
     The word is, " Stay," says ever, " Come."
          O show Thyself to me,
          Or take me up to Thee !

THE BRITISH CHURCH

I JOY, dear Mother, when I view
Thy perfect lineaments, and hue
      Both sweet and bright:
Beauty in thee takes up her place,
And dates her letters from thy face,
      When she doth write.

A fine aspect in fit array,
Neither too mean, nor yet too gay,
      Shows who is best:
Outlandish looks may not compare;
For all they either painted are,
      Or else undrest.

She on the hills, which wantonly
Allureth all in hope to be
      By her preferred,
Hath kissed so long her painted shrines,
That e'en her face by kissing shines,
      For her reward.

She in the valley is so shy
Of dressing, that her hair doth lie
      About her ears:
While she avoids her neighbour's pride,
She wholly goes on the other side,
      And nothing wears.

But, dearest Mother, (what those miss)
The mean thy praise and glory is,
      And long may be.
Blessed be God, whose love it was
To double-moat thee with His grace,
      And none but thee.

THE QUIP

THE merry world did on a day
   With his train-bands and mates agree
To meet together, where I lay,
And all in sport to jeer at me.

First, beauty crept into a rose;
Which when I pluckt not, Sir, said she,
Tell me, I pray, whose hands are those?
But Thou shalt answer, Lord, for me.

Then money came, and chinking still,
What tune is this, poor man? said he:
I heard in music you had skill:
But Thou shalt answer, Lord, for me.

Then came brave glory puffing by
In silks that whistled, who but he!
He scarce allowed me half an eye:
But Thou shalt answer, Lord, for me.

Then came quick wit and conversation,
And he would needs a comfort be,
And, to be short, make an oration,
But Thou shalt answer, Lord, for me.

Yet when the hour of Thy design
To answer these fine things shall come;
Speak not at large, say, I am Thine,
And then they have their answer home.

VANITY

POOR silly soul, whose hope and head lies low;
  Whose flat delights on earth do creep and grow:
To whom the stars shine not so fair, as eyes;
Nor solid work, as false embroideries;
Hark and beware, lest what you now do measure,
And write for sweet, prove a most sour displeasure.

  O hear betimes, lest thy relenting
      May come too late!
  To purchase heaven for repenting
      Is no hard rate.
  If souls be made of earthly mould,
      Let them love gold;
      If born on high,
  Let them unto their kindred fly:
  For they can never be at rest,
  Till they regain their ancient nest.
Then silly soul, take heed; for earthly joy
Is but a bubble, and makes thee a boy.

THE DAWNING

AWAKE sad heart, whom sorrow ever drowns:
  Take up thine eyes, which feed on earth,
Unfold thy forehead gathered into frowns:
  Thy Saviour comes, and with Him mirth:
      Awake, awake;
And with a thankful heart His comforts take.
  But thou dost still lament, and pine, and cry;
  And feel His death, but not His victory.

Arise sad heart; if thou dost not withstand,
    Christ's resurrection thine may be:
Do not by hanging down break from the hand,
    Which, as it riseth, raiseth thee:
                Arise, arise;
And with His burial linen dry thine eyes.
    Christ left His grave-clothes, that we might, when grief
    Draws tears, or blood, not want an handkerchief.

JESU

JESU is in my heart, His sacred name
    Is deeply carved there; but the other week
A great affliction broke the little frame,
E'en all to pieces; which I went to seek:
And first I found the corner where was I,
After, where ES, and next where U was graved.
When I had got these parcels, instantly
I sat me down to spell them, and perceived
That to my broken heart He was I EASE YOU,
         And to my whole is *JESU*.

BUSINESS

CANST be idle? canst thou play,
    Foolish soul who sinned to-day?

Rivers run, and springs each one
Know their home, and get them gone:
Hast thou tears, or hast thou none?

If, poor soul, thou hast no tears,
Would thou hadst no faults or fears!
Who hath these, those ills forbears.

Winds still work: it is their plot,
Be the season cold or hot:
Hast thou sighs, or hast thou not?

If thou hast no sighs or groans,
Would thou hadst no flesh and bones!
Lesser pains scape greater ones.

But if yet thou idle be,
Foolish soul, Who died for thee?

Who did leave His Father's throne,
To assume thy flesh and bone?
Had He life, or had He none?

If He had not lived for thee,
Thou hadst died most wretchedly;
And two deaths had been thy fee.

He so far thy good did plot,
That His own self He forgot.
Did He die, or did He not?

If He had not died for thee,
Thou hadst lived in misery.
Two lives worse than ten deaths be.

And hath any space of breath
'Twixt his sins and Saviour's death?

He that loseth gold, though dross,
Tells to all he meets his cross :
He that sins, hath he no loss?

He that finds a silver vein,
Thinks on it, and thinks again :
Brings thy Saviour's death no gain ?

Who in heart not ever kneels,
Neither sin nor Saviour feels.

DIALOGUE

SWEETEST Saviour, if my soul
Were but worth the having,
Quickly should I then control
Any thought of waving.
But when all my care and pains
Cannot give the name of gains
To Thy wretch so full of stains;
What delight or hope remains?

What (Child), is the balance thine ?
Thine the poise and measure ?
If I say ' Thou shalt be Mine,'
Finger not My treasure.
What the gains in having thee
Do amount to, only He,
Who for man was sold, can see,
That transferred the accounts to me.

But as I can see no merit,
Leading to this favour :

So the way to fit me for it,
    Is beyond my savour.
As the reason then is Thine;
So the way is none of mine:
I disclaim the whole design:
Sin disclaims and I resign.

That is all, if that I could
    Get without repining;
And My clay, My creature, would
    Follow My resigning:
That as I did freely part
With My glory and desert,
Left all joys to feel all smart——
Ah! no more: Thou break'st my heart.

DULNESS

WHY do I languish thus, drooping and dull,
    As if I were all earth?
O give me quickness, that I may with mirth
    Praise Thee brimful!

The wanton lover in a curious strain
    Can praise his fairest fair;
And with quaint metaphors her curled hair
    Curl o'er again:

Thou art my loveliness, my life, my light,
    Beauty alone to me:
Thy bloody death, and undeserved, makes Thee
    Pure red and white.

When all perfections as but one appear,
    That those Thy form doth show,
The very dust, where Thou dost tread and go
    Makes beauties here;

Where are my lines then? my approaches? views?
    Where are my window-songs?
Lovers are still pretending, and e'en wrongs
    Sharpen their muse,

But I am lost in flesh, whose sugared lies
    Still mock me, and grow bold:
Sure Thou didst put a mind there, if I could
    Find where it lies.

Lord, clear Thy gift, that with a constant wit
    I may but look towards Thee:
Look only; for to love Thee, who can be,
    What angel, fit?

LOVE-JOY

AS on a window late I cast mine eye,
    I saw a vine drop grapes with J and C
Annealed on every bunch.   One standing by
Asked what it meant.   I (who am never loth
To spend my judgment) said, it seemed to me
To be the body and the letters both
Of Joy and Charity.   Sir, you have not missed,
The man replied; It figures *JESUS CHRIST*.

PROVIDENCE

O SACRED Providence, Who from end to end
    Strongly and sweetly movest! shall I write,
And not of Thee, through whom my fingers bend
To hold my quill? shall they not do Thee right?

Of all the creatures both in sea and land,
Only to man Thou hast made known Thy ways,
And put the pen alone into his hand,
And made him secretary of Thy praise.

Beasts fain would sing; birds ditty to their notes;
Trees would be tuning on their native lute
To Thy renown: but all their hands and throats
Are brought to man, while they are lame and mute.

Man is the world's high priest: he doth present
The sacrifice for all; while they below
Unto the service mutter an assent,
Such as springs use that fall, and winds that blow.

He that to praise and laud Thee doth refrain,
Doth not refrain unto himself alone,
But robs a thousand who would praise Thee fain;
And doth commit a world of sin in one.

The beasts say, eat me; but, if beasts must teach,
The tongue is yours to eat, but mine to praise.
The trees say, pull me: but the hand you stretch
Is mine to write, as it is yours to raise.

Wherefore, most sacred Spirit, I here present
For me and all my fellows praise to Thee:
And just it is that I should pay the rent,
Because the benefit accrues to me.

We all acknowledge both Thy power and love
To be exact, transcendent, and divine;
Who dost so strongly and so sweetly move,
While all things have their will, yet none but Thine

For either Thy command, or Thy permission
Lay hands on all: they are Thy right and left.
The first puts on with speed and expedition;
The other curbs sin's stealing pace and theft;

Nothing escapes them both: all must appear,
And be disposed, and dressed, and tuned by Thee,
Who sweetly temperest all.   If we could hear
Thy skill and art, what music would it be!

Thou art in small things great, not small in any:
Thy even praise can neither rise, nor fall.
Thou art in all things one, in each thing many:
For Thou art infinite in one, and all.

Tempests are calm to Thee, they know Thy hand,
And hold it fast, as children do their father's,
Which cry and follow.   Thou hast made poor sand
Check the proud sea, e'en when it swells and gathers.

Thy cupboard serves the world: the meat is set
Where all may reach: no beast but knows his feed.
Birds teach us hawking: fishes have their net:
The great prey on the less, they on some weed.

Nothing engendered doth prevent his meat;
Flies have their table spread, ere they appear;
Some creatures have in winter what to eat;
Others do sleep, and envy not their cheer.

How finely dost Thou times and seasons spin,
And make a twist checkered with night and day!
Which as it lengthens, winds, and winds us in,
As bowls go on, but turning all the way.

Each creature hath a wisdom for his good.
The pigeons feed their tender offspring, crying,
When they are callow; but withdraw their food,
When they are fledged, that need may teach them
    flying.

Bees work for man; and yet they never bruise
Their master's flower, but leave it, having done,
As fair as ever, and as fit for use:
So both the flower doth stay, and honey run.

Sheep eat the grass, and dung the ground for more:
Trees after bearing drop their leaves for soil:
Springs vent their streams, and by expense get store:
Clouds cool by heat, and baths by cooling boil.

Who hath the virtue to express the rare
And curious virtues both of herbs and stones?
Is there an herb for that? O that Thy care
Would show a root, that gives expressions!

And if an herb hath power, what have the stars?
A rose, besides his beauty, is a cure.
Doubtless our plagues and plenty, peace and wars,
Are there much surer than our art is sure.

Thou hast hid metals: man may take them thence;
But at his peril: when he digs the place,
He makes a grave; as if the thing had sense,
And threatened man, that he should fill the space.

E'en poisons praise Thee.   Should a thing be lost?
Should creatures want, for want of heed, their due?
Since where are poisons, antidotes are most;
The help stands close, and keeps the fear in view.

The sea, which seems to stop the traveller,
Is by a ship the speedier passage made.
The winds, who think they rule the mariner,
Are ruled by him, and taught to serve his trade.

And as Thy house is full, so I adore
Thy curious art in marshalling Thy goods.
The hills with health abound, the vales with store;
The south with marble; north with furs and woods.

Hard things are glorious; easy things good cheap;
The common all men have; that which is rare,
Men therefore seek to have, and care to keep.
The healthy frosts with summer fruits compare.

Light without wind is glass: warm without weight
Is wool and furs: cool without closeness, shade:
Speed without pains, a horse: tall without height,
A servile hawk: low without loss, a spade.

All countries have enough to serve their need:
If they seek fine things, Thou dost make them run
For their offence; and then dost turn their speed
To be commerce and trade from sun to sun.

Nothing wears clothes, but man; nothing doth need
But he to wear them.   Nothing useth fire,
But man alone, to show his heavenly breed:
And only he hath fuel in desire.

When the earth was dry, Thou madest a sea of wet:
When that lay gathered, Thou didst broach the
    mountains:
When yet some places could no moisture get,
The winds grew gardeners, and the clouds good
    fountains.

Rain, do not hurt my flowers; but gently spend
Your honey drops: press not to smell them here;
When they are ripe, their odour will ascend,
And at your lodging with their thanks appear.

How harsh are thorns to pears! and yet they make
A better hedge, and need less reparation.
How smooth are silks, compared with a stake,
Or with a stone! yet make no good foundation.

Sometimes Thou dost divide thy gifts to man,
Sometimes unite.   The Indian nut alone
Is clothing, meat and trencher, drink and can,
Boat, cable, sail and needle, all in one.

Most herbs that grow in brooks are hot and dry.
Cold fruit's warm kernels help against the wind.
The lemon's juice and rind cure mutually.
The whey of milk doth loose, the milk doth bind.

Thy creatures leap not, but express a feast,
Where all the guests sit close, and nothing wants.
Frogs marry fish and flesh; bats, bird and beast;
Sponges, non-sense and sense; mines, the earth and
    plants.

To show Thou art not bound, as if Thy lot
Were worse than ours, sometimes Thou shiftest hands.
Most things move the under jaw; the crocodile not,
Most things sleep lying, the elephant leans or stands.

But who hath praise enough? nay, who hath any?
None can express Thy works, but he that knows them;
And none can know Thy works, which are so many,
And so complete, but only he that owes them.

All things that are, though they have several ways,
Yet in their being join with one advice
To honour Thee: and so I give Thee praise
In all my other hymns, but in this twice.

Each thing that is, although in use and name
It go for one, hath many ways in store
To honour Thee; and so each hymn Thy fame
Extolleth many ways, yet this one more.

HOPE

I GAVE to Hope a watch of mine: but he
      An anchor gave to me.
Then an old Prayer-book I did present:
      And he an optic sent.
With that I gave a phial full of tears:
      But he a few green ears.
Ah, loiterer! I'll no more, no more I'll bring:
      I did expect a ring.

SIN'S ROUND

SORRY I am, my God, sorry I am,
   That my offences course it in a ring.
My thoughts are working like a busy flame,
Until their cockatrice they hatch and bring:
And when they once have perfected their draughts,
My words take fire from my inflamed thoughts.

My words take fire from my inflamed thoughts,
Which spit it forth like the Sicilian hill.
They vent the wares, and pass them with their faults,
And by their breathing ventilate the ill.
But words suffice not, where are lewd intentions:
My hands do join to finish the inventions:

My hands do join to finish the inventions:
And so my sins ascend three stories high,
As Babel grew, before there were dissensions.
Yet ill deeds loiter not: for they supply
New thoughts of sinning; wherefore, to my shame,
Sorry I am, my God, sorry I am.

TIME

MEETING with Time, Slack thing, said I,
   Thy scythe is dull; whet it for shame.
No marvel, Sir, he did reply,
If it at length deserve some blame:
   But where one man would have me grind it,
   Twenty for one too sharp do find it.

Perhaps some such of old did pass,
Who above all things loved this life;
To whom thy scythe a hatchet was,
Which now is but a pruning-knife.
    Christ's coming hath made man thy debtor,
    Since by thy cutting he grows better.

And in His blessing thou art blest:
For where thou only wert before
An executioner at best,
Thou art a gardener now, and more.
    An usher to convey our souls
    Beyond the utmost stars and poles.

And this is that makes life so long,
While it detains us from our God.
E'en pleasures here increase the wrong:
And length of days lengthen the rod.
    Who wants the place, where God doth dwell,
    Partakes already half of hell.

Of what strange length must that needs be,
Which e'en eternity excludes!
Thus far Time heard me patiently:
Then chafing said, this man deludes:
    What do I hear before his door?
    He doth not crave less time, but more.

GRATEFULNESS

THOU that hast given so much to me,
    Give one thing more, a grateful heart.
See how Thy beggar works on Thee
        By art.

He makes Thy gifts occasion more,
And says, if he in this be crost,
All Thou hast given him heretofore
         Is lost.

But Thou didst reckon, when at first
Thy word our hearts and hands did crave,
What it would come to at the worst
         To save.

Perpetual knockings at Thy door,
Tears sullying Thy transparent rooms,
Gift upon gift; much would have more,
         And comes.

This notwithstanding, Thou went'st on,
And didst allow us all our noise:
Nay Thou hast made a sigh and groan
         Thy joys.

Not that Thou hast not still above
Much better tunes, than groans can make;
But that these country-airs Thy love
         Did take.

Wherefore I cry, and cry again;
And in no quiet canst Thou be,
Till I a thankful heart obtain
         Of Thee:

Not thankful, when it pleaseth me;
As if Thy blessings had spare days:
But such a heart, whose pulse may be
         Thy praise.

PEACE

SWEET Peace, where dost thou dwell? I humbly
    crave,
      Let me once know.
I sought thee in a secret cave,
    And asked, if Peace were there.
A hollow wind did seem to answer, no:
      Go seek elsewhere.

I did; and going did a rainbow note:
      Surely, thought I,
This is the lace of Peace's coat:
    I will search out the matter.
But while I looked, the clouds immediately
      Did break and scatter.

Then went I to a garden, and did spy
    A gallant flower,
The crown imperial: Sure, said I,
    Peace at the root must dwell.
But when I digged, I saw a worm devour
    What showed so well.

At length I met a reverend good old man:
    Whom when for Peace
I did demand, he thus began;
    There was a Prince of old
At Salem dwelt, Who lived with good increase
    Of flock and fold.

He sweetly lived; yet sweetness did not save
    His life from foes.
But after death out of His grave

There sprang twelve stalks of wheat:
Which many wondering at, got some of those
        To plant and set.

It prospered strangely, and did soon disperse
        Through all the earth:
    For they that taste it do rehearse,
        That virtue lies therein;
A secret virtue, bringing peace and mirth
        By flight of sin.

Take of this grain, which in my garden grows,
        And grows for you;
    Make bread of it: and that repose
        And peace, which everywhere
With so much earnestness you do pursue
        Is only there.

CONFESSION

O WHAT a cunning guest
    Is this same grief! within my heart I made
    Closets; and in them many a chest;
    And like a master in my trade,
In those chests, boxes; in each box, a till:
Yet grief knows all, and enters when he will.

    No screw, no piercer can
Into a piece of timber work and wind,
    As God's afflictions into man.
    When He a torture hath designed.
They are too subtle for the subtlest hearts;
And fall, like rheums, upon the tenderest parts.

We are the earth; and they,
Like moles within us, heave, and cast about:
     And till they foot and clutch their prey,
     They never cool, much less give out.
No smith can make such locks, but they have keys:
Closets are halls to them; and hearts, highways.

     Only an open breast
Doth shut them out, so that they cannot enter;
     Or, if they enter, cannot rest,
     But quickly seek some new adventure.
Smooth open hearts no fastening have; but fiction
Doth give a hold and handle to affliction.

     Wherefore my faults and sins,
Lord, I acknowledge; take Thy plagues away:
     For since confession pardon wins,
     I challenge here the brightest day,
The clearest diamond: let them do their best,
They shall be thick and cloudy to my breast.

GIDDINESS

O WHAT a thing is man! how far from power,
     From settled peace and rest!
He is some twenty several men at least
     Each several hour.

One while he counts of heaven, as of his treasure:
     But then a thought creeps in,
And calls him coward, who for fear of sin
     Will lose a pleasure.

Now he will fight it out, and to the wars;
    Now eat his bread in peace,
And snudge in quiet: now he scorns increase;
    Now all day spares.

He builds a house, which quickly down must go,
    As if a whirlwind blew
And crushed the building: and 'tis partly true,
    His mind is so.

O what a sight were man, if his attires
    Did alter with his mind;
And, like a dolphin's skin, his clothes combined
    With his desires!

Surely if each one saw another's heart,
    There would be no commerce,
No sale or bargain pass: all would disperse,
    And live apart.

Lord, mend or rather make us: one creation
    Will not suffice our turn:
Except Thou make us daily, we shall spurn
    Our own salvation.

THE BUNCH OF GRAPES

JOY, I did lock thee up: but some bad man
    Hath let thee out again:
And now, methinks, I am where I began
    Seven years ago: one vogue and vein,
    One air of thoughts usurps my brain;

I did towards Canaan draw; but now I am
Brought back to the Red Sea, the sea of shame.

For as the Jews of old by God's command
        Travelled, and saw no town;
So now each Christian hath his journeys spanned:
        Their story pens and sets us down.
        A single deed is small renown.
God's works are wide, and let in future times;
His ancient justice overflows our crimes.

Then have we too our guardian fires and clouds;
        Our scripture-dew drops fast:
We have our sands and serpents, tents and shrouds:
        Alas! our murmurings come not last.
        But where's the cluster? where's the taste
Of mine inheritance? Lord, if I must borrow,
Let me as well take up their joy, as sorrow.

But can he want the grape, who hath the wine?
     .   I have their fruit and more.
Blessed be God, who prospered Noah's vine,
        And made it bring forth grapes good store.
        But much more Him I must adore,
Who of the law's sour juice sweet wine did make,
E'en God Himself being pressed for my sake.

LOVE UNKNOWN

DEAR friend, sit down, the tale is long and sad:
    And in my faintings I presume your love
Will more comply, than help. A Lord I had,
And have, of Whom some grounds, which may im-
    prove,

I hold for two lives, and both lives in me.
To Him I brought a dish of fruit one day,
And in the middle placed my heart.   But He
     (I sigh to say)
Looked on a servant, who did know His eye
Better than you know me, or (which is one)
Than I myself.   The servant instantly
Quitting the fruit, seized on my heart alone,
And threw it in a font, wherein did fall
A stream of blood, which issued from the side
Of a great rock: I well remember all,
And have good cause: there it was dipt and dyed,
And washed, and wrung: the very wringing yet
Enforceth tears.
    "Your heart was foul, I fear."
Indeed 'tis true.   I did and do commit
Many a fault more than my lease will bear;
Yet still asked pardon, and was not denied.
But you shall hear.   After my heart was well,
And clean and fair, as I one eventide
     (I sigh to tell)
Walked by myself abroad, I saw a large
And spacious furnace flaming, and thereon
A boiling caldron, round about whose verge
Was in great letters set *AFFLICTION*.
The greatness showed the Owner.   So I went
To fetch a sacrifice out of my fold,
Thinking with that, which I did thus present,
To warm His love, which I did fear grew cold.
But as my heart did tender it, the man
Who was to take it from me, slipt his hand,
And threw my heart into the scalding pan ;
My heart that brought it (do you understand?)
The offerer's heart.
    "Your heart was hard, I fear."
Indeed 'tis true.   I found a callous matter

Began to spread and to expatiate there :
But with a richer drug than scalding water
I bathed it often, e'en with holy blood,
Which at a board, while many drank bare wine,
A friend did steal into my cup for good,
E'en taken inwardly, and most divine
To supple hardnesses.   But at the length
Out of the caldron getting, soon I fled
Unto my house, where to repair the strength
Which I had lost, I hasted to my bed :
But when I thought to sleep out all these faults,
                          (I sigh to speak)
I found that some had stuffed the bed with thoughts,
I would say thorns.   Dear, could my heart not break,
When with my pleasures e'en my rest was gone?
Full well I understood Who had been there :
For I had given the key to none, but One :
It must be He.
                     " Your heart was dull, I fear."
Indeed a slack and sleepy state of mind
Did oft possess me, so that when I prayed,
Though my lips went, my heart did stay behind.
But all my scores were by another paid,
Who took the debt upon Him.
                              " Truly, friend,
" For ought I hear, your Master shows to you
" More favour than you wot of.   Mark the end.
" The font did only what was old renew :
" The caldron suppled what was grown too hard :
" The thorns did quicken what was grown too dull:
" All did but strive to mend what you had marred.
" Wherefore be cheered, and praise Him to the full
" Each day, each hour, each moment of the week,
" Who fain would have you be, new, tender, quick."

MAN'S MEDLEY

HARK, how the birds do sing,
        And woods do ring.
All creatures have their joy, and man hath his.
     Yet if we rightly measure,
        Man's joy and pleasure
Rather hereafter, than in present, is.

     To this life things of sense
        Make their pretence :
In the other Angels have a right by birth :
     Man ties them both alone,
        And makes them one,
With the one hand touching heaven, with the other
   earth.

     In soul he mounts and flies,
        In flesh he dies.
He wears a stuff whose thread is coarse and round,
     But trimmed with curious lace,
        And should take place
After the trimming, not the stuff and ground.

     Not, that he may not here
        Taste of the cheer :
But as birds drink, and straight lift up their head ;
     So must he sip, and think
        Of better drink
He may attain to, after he is dead.

     But as his joys are double,
        So is his trouble.

He hath two winters, other things but one :
      Both frosts and thoughts do nip,
          And bite his lip ;
And he of all things fears two deaths alone.

      Yet even the greatest griefs
          May be reliefs,
Could he but take them right, and in their ways.
      Happy is he, whose heart
          Hath found the art
To turn his double pains to double praise.

THE· STORM

I F as the winds and waters here below
          Do fly and flow,
My sighs and tears as busy were above;
          Sure they would move
And much affect Thee, as tempestuous times
Amaze poor mortals, and object their crimes.

Stars have their storms, even in a high degree,
          As well as we.
A throbbing conscience spurred by remorse
          Hath a strange force:
It quits the earth, and mounting more and more,
Dares to assault Thee, and besiege Thy door.

There it stands knocking, to thy music's wrong,
          And drowns the song.
Glory and honour are set by, till it
          An answer get,
Poets have wronged poor storms: such days are best;
They purge the air without, within the breast.

PARADISE

I BLESS Thee, Lord, because I GROW
Among Thy trees, which in a ROW
To Thee both fruit and order OW.

What open force, or hidden CHARM
Can blast my fruit, or bring me HARM,
While the inclosure is Thine ARM?

Inclose me still for fear I START.
Be to me rather sharp and TART,
Than let me want Thy hand and ART.

When Thou dost greater judgments SPARE,
And with Thy knife but prune and PARE,
E'en fruitful trees more fruitful ARE.

Such sharpness shows the sweetest FRIEND:
Such cuttings rather heal than REND:
And such beginnings touch their END.

THE METHOD

POOR heart, lament.
For since thy God refuseth still,
There is some rub, some discontent,
Which cools His will.

Thy Father could
Quickly effect, what thou dost move;
For He is Power: and sure He would:
For He is Love.

Go search this thing,
Tumble thy breast, and turn thy book:
If thou hadst lost a glove or ring,
    Wouldst thou not look?

What do I see
Written above there? "Yesterday
"I did behave me carelessly,
    "When I did pray."

And should God's ear
To such indifferents chained be,
Who do not their own motions hear?
    Is God less free?

But stay! what's there?
"Late when I would have something done,
"I had a motion to forbear,
    "Yet I went on."

And should God's ear,
Which needs not man, be tied to those
Who hear not Him, but quickly hear
    His utter foes;

Then once more pray:
Down with thy knees, up with thy voice:
Seek pardon first, and God will say,
    "Glad heart, rejoice."

DIVINITY

AS men, for fear the stars should sleep and nod,
　　And trip at night, have spheres supplied;
As if a star were duller than a clod
　Which knows his way without a guide:

Just so the other heaven they also serve,
　　Divinity's transcendent sky:
Which with the edge of wit they cut and carve.
　　Reason triumphs, and Faith lies by.

Could not that Wisdom, which first broached the wine,
　　Have thickened it with definitions:
And jagged His seamless coat, had that been fine,
　　With curious questions and divisions?

But all the doctrine, which He taught and gave,
　　Was clear as heaven, from whence it came.
At least those beams of truth, which only save,
　　Surpass in brightness any flame.

"Love God, and love your neighbour. Watch and
　　　pray.
　"Do as you would be done unto."
O dark instructions, e'en as dark as day!
　　Who can these Gordian knots undo?

But He doth bid us take His blood for wine.
　　Bid what He please; yet I am sure,
To take and taste what He doth there design,
　　Is all that saves, and not obscure.

Then burn thy Epicycles, foolish man;
    Break all thy spheres, and save thy head;
Faith needs no staff of flesh, but stoutly can
    To heaven alone both go and lead.

GRIEVE NOT THE HOLY SPIRIT, ETC.

EPHES. iv. 30.

AND art Thou grieved, sweet and sacred Dove,
    When I am sour
    And cross Thy love?
Grieved for me? the God of strength and power
    Grieved for a worm, which when I tread
    I pass away and leave it dead?

Then weep, mine eyes, the God of love doth grieve:
    Weep, foolish heart,
    And weeping live; .
For death is dry as dust. Yet if we part,
    End as the night, whose sable hue
    Your sins express; melt into dew.

When saucy mirth shall knock or call at door,
    Cry out, get hence,
    Or cry no more.
Almighty God doth grieve, He puts on sense:
    I sin not to my grief alone,
    But to my God's too; He doth groan.

O take thy lute, and tune it to a strain,
    Which may with thee
    All day complain.
There can no discord but in ceasing be.

Marbles can weep; and surely strings
More bowels have, than such hard things.

Lord, I adjudge myself to tears and grief,
E'en endless tears
Without relief.
If a clear spring for me no time forbears,
But runs, although I be not dry;
I am no crystal, what shall I?

Yet if I wail not still, since still to wail
Nature denies;
And flesh would fail,
If my deserts were masters of mine eyes:
Lord, pardon, for Thy Son makes good
My want of tears with store of blood.

THE FAMILY

WHAT doth this noise of thoughts within my
heart,
As if they had a part?
What do these loud complaints and puling fears,
As if there were no rule or ears?

But, Lord, the house and family are Thine,
Though some of them repine.
Turn out these wranglers, which defile Thy seat:
For where Thou dwellest all is neat.

First peace and silence all disputes control,
Then order plays the soul;
And giving all things their set forms and hours,
Makes of wild woods sweet walks and bowers.

Humble obedience near the door doth stand,
Expecting a command :
Than whom in waiting nothing seems more slow,
Nothing more quick when she doth go.

Joys oft are there, and griefs as oft as joys ;
But griefs without a noise :
Yet speak they louder than distempered fears :
What is so shrill as silent tears ?

This is Thy house, with these it doth abound :
And where these are not found,
Perhaps Thou comest sometimes, and for a day ;
But not to make a constant stay.

THE SIZE

CONTENT thee, greedy heart.
Modest and moderate joys to those, that have
Title to more hereafter when they part,
Are passing brave.
Let the upper springs into the low
Descend and fall, and thou dost flow.

What though some have a fraught
Of cloves and nutmegs, and in cinnamon sail?
If thou hast wherewithal to spice a draught,
When griefs prevail,
And for the future time art heir
To the isle of spices, is't not fair?

To be in both worlds full
Is more than God was, Who was hungry here.
Wouldst thou His laws of fasting disannul?
      Enact good cheer?
Lay out thy joy, yet hope to save it?
Wouldst thou both eat thy cake, and have it?

Great joys are all at once;
But little do reserve themselves for more:
Those have their hopes; these what they have re-
      And live on score: [nounce,
Those are at home; these journey still,
And meet the rest on Sion's hill.

Thy Saviour sentenced joy,
And in the flesh condemned it as unfit,
At least in lump: for such doth oft destroy;
      Whereas a bit
Doth 'tice us on to hopes of more,
And for the present health restore.

A Christian's state and case
Is not a corpulent, but a thin and spare,
Yet active strength: whose long and bony face
      Content and care
Do seem to equally divide,
Like a pretender, not a bride.

Wherefore sit down, good heart;
Grasp not at much, for fear thou losest all.
If comforts fell according to desert,
      They would great frosts and snows destroy:
For we should count, since the last joy.

Then close again the seam
Which thou hast opened; do not spread thy robe
In hope of great things.   Call to mind thy dream,
An earthly globe,
On whose meridian was engraven,
" These seas are tears, and Heaven the haven."

ARTILLERY

AS I one evening sat before my cell,
Methought a star did shoot into my lap.
I rose, and shook my clothes, as knowing well,
That from small fire comes oft no small mishap:
When suddenly I heard one say,
" Do as thou usest, disobey,
" Expel good motions from thy breast,
" Which have the face of fire, but end in rest."

I, who had heard of music in the spheres,
But not of speech in stars, began to muse:
But turning to my God, Whose ministers
The stars and all things are; if I refuse,
Dread Lord, said I, so oft my good;
Then I refuse not e'en with blood
To wash away my stubborn thought:
For I will do, or suffer what I ought.

But I have also stars and shooters too,
Born where Thy servants both artilleries use.
My tears and prayers night and day do woo,
And work up to Thee; yet Thou dost refuse.

Not but I am (I must say still)
Much more obliged to do Thy will,
Than Thou to grant mine : but because
Thy promise now hath e'en set Thee Thy laws.

Then we are shooters both, and Thou dost deign
To enter combat with us, and contest
With Thine own clay.   But I would parley fain :
Shun not my arrows, and behold my breast.
    Yet if Thou shunnest, I am Thine :
    I must be so, if I am mine.
    There is no articling with Thee :
I am but finite, yet Thine infinitely.

CHURCH-RENTS AND SCHISMS

BRAVE rose (alas!) where art thou? in the chair,
    Where thou didst lately so triumph and shine,
A worm doth sit, whose many feet and hair
Are the more foul, the more thou wert divine.
This, this hath done it, this did bite the root
And bottom of the leaves: which when the wind
Did once perceive, it blew them under foot
Where rude unhallowed steps do crush and grind
    Their beauteous glories.   Only shreds of thee,
    And those all bitten, in thy chair I see.

Why doth my Mother blush? is she the rose,
And shows it so?   Indeed Christ's precious blood
Gave you a colour once; which when your foes
Thought to let out, the bleeding did you good,
And made you look much fresher than before.
But when debates and fretting jealousies

Did worm and work within you more and more,
Your colour faded, and calamities
    Turned your ruddy into pale and bleak:
    Your health and beauty both began to break.

Then did your several parts unloose and start:
Which when your neighbours saw, like a north wind
They rushed in and cast them in the dirt
Where Pagans tread.   O Mother dear and kind,
Where shall I get me eyes enough to weep,
As many eyes as stars? since it is night,
And much of Asia and Europe fast asleep,
And e'en all Afric; would at least I might
    With these two poor ones lick up all the dew,
    Which falls by night, and pour it out for you!

JUSTICE (—)

O DREADFUL justice, what a fright and terror
        Wast thou of old,
        When sin and error
    Did show and shape thy looks to me,
      And through their glass discolour thee!
He that did but look up, was proud and bold.

The dishes of thy balance seemed to gape,
        Like two great pits;
        The beam and scape
    Did like some tottering engine show:
      Thy hand above did burn and glow,
Daunting the stoutest hearts, the proudest wits.

But now that Christ's pure veil presents the sight,
I see no fears:
Thy hand is white,
Thy scales like buckets, which attend
And interchangeably descend,
Lifting to heaven from this well of tears.

For where before thou still didst call on me,
Now I still touch
And harp on thee.
God's promises have made thee mine:
Why should I justice now decline?
Against me there is none, but for me much.

THE PILGRIMAGE

I TRAVELLED on, seeing the hill, where lay
My expectation.
A long it was and weary way.
The gloomy cave of Desperation
I left on the one, and on the other side
The rock of Pride.

And so I came to Fancy's meadow strowed
With many a flower:
Fain would I here have made abode,
But I was quickened by my hour.
So to Care's copse I came, and there got through
With much ado.

That led me to the wild of Passion; which
Some call the wold;
A wasted place, but sometimes rich.
Here I was robbed of all my gold.

Save one good Angel, which a friend had tied
                Close to my side.

At length I got unto the gladsome hill,
                Where lay my hope,
Where lay my heart; and climbing still,
        When I had gained the brow and top,   .
A lake of brackish waters on the ground
                Was all I found.

With that abashed, and struck with many a sting
                Of swarming fears,
        I fell, and cried, Alas, my King!
        Can both the way and end be tears?
Yet taking heart I rose, and then perceived
                I was deceived:

My hill was further: so I flung away,
                Yet heard a cry
        Just as I went, "none goes that way
        And lives:" if that be all, said I,
After so foul a journey death is fair,
                And but a chair.

THE HOLD-FAST

I THREATENED to observe the strict decree
    Of my dear God with all my power and might:
But I was told by one, it could not be;
Yet I might trust in God to be my light.

Then will I trust, said I, in Him alone.
    Nay, e'en to trust in Him, was also His:
    We must confess, that nothing is our own.
Then I confess that He my succour is:

But to have nought is ours, not to confess
    That we have nought.   I stood amazed at this,
    Much troubled, till I heard a friend express,
That all things were more ours by being His.
    What Adam had, and forfeited for all,
    Christ keepeth now, Who cannot fail or fall.

COMPLAINING

DO not beguile my heart,
    Because Thou art
My power and wisdom.   Put me not to shame,
    Because I am
Thy clay that weeps, Thy dust that calls.

Thou art the Lord of glory;
    The deed and story
Are both Thy due: but I a silly fly,
    That live or die,
According as the weather falls.

Art thou all justice, Lord?
    Shows not thy word
More attributes?   Am I all throat or eye,
    To weep or cry?
Have I no parts but those of grief?

Let not Thy wrathful power
Afflict my hour,
My inch of life: or let Thy gracious power
Contract my hour,
That I may climb and find relief.

THE DISCHARGE

BUSY enquiring heart, what wouldst thou know?
Why dost thou pry,
And turn, and leer, and with a licorous eye
Look high and low;
And in thy lookings stretch and grow?

Hast thou not made thy counts, and summed up all?
Did not thy heart
Give up the whole, and with the whole depart?
Let what will fall:
That which is past who can recall?

Thy life is God's, thy time to come is gone,
And is His right.
He is thy night at noon: He is at night
Thy noon alone.
The crop is His, for He hath sown.

And well it was for thee, when this befell,
That God did make
Thy business His, and in thy life partake:
For thou canst tell,
If it be His once, all is well.

Only the present is thy part and fee.
And happy thou,
If, though thou didst not beat thy future brow,
Thou couldst well see
What present things required of thee.

They ask enough; why shouldst thou further go?
Raise not the mud
Of future depths, but drink the clear and good.
Dig not for woe
In times to come; for it will grow.

Man and the present fit: if he provide,
He breaks the square.
This hour is mine: if for the next I care,
I grow too wide,
And do encroach upon death's side:

For death each hour environs and surrounds.
He that would know
And care for future chances, cannot go
Unto those grounds,
But through a churchyard which them bounds.

Things present shrink and die: but they that spend
Their thoughts and sense
On future grief, do not remove it thence,
But it extend,
And draw the bottom out an end.

God chains the dog till night: wilt loose the chain,
And wake thy sorrow?
Wilt thou forestall it, and now grieve to-morrow,
And then again
Grieve over freshly all thy pain?

Either grief will not come: or if it must,
Do not forecast:
And while it cometh, it is almost past.
Away distrust:
My God hath promised; He is just.

PRAISE

KING of glory, King of peace,
I will love Thee:
And that love may never cease,
I will move Thee.

Thou hast granted my request,
Thou hast heard me:
Thou didst note my working breast,
Thou hast spared me.

Wherefore with my utmost art
I will sing Thee,
And the cream of all my heart
I will bring Thee.

Though my sins against me cried,
Thou didst clear me;
And alone, when they replied,
Thou didst hear me.

Seven whole days, not one in seven,
I will praise Thee.
In my heart, though not in Heaven,
I can raise Thee.

Thou grewest soft and moist with tears,
  Thou relentedst.
And when justice called for fears,
  Thou dissentedst.

Small it is, in this poor sort
  To enrol Thee :
E'en eternity is too short
  To extol Thee.

AN OFFERING

COME, bring thy gift. If blessings were as slow
 As men's returns, what would become of fools?
What hast thou there? a heart? but is it pure?
Search well and see ; for hearts have many holes.
Yet one pure heart is nothing to bestow :
In Christ two natures met to be thy cure.

O that within us hearts had propagation,
Since many gifts do challenge many hearts !
Yet one, if good, may title to a number ;
And single things grow fruitful by deserts.
In public judgments one may be a nation,
And fence a plague, while others sleep and slumber.

But all I fear is, lest thy heart displease,
As neither good, nor one : so oft divisions
Thy lusts have made, and not thy lusts alone ;
Thy passions also have their set partitions.
These parcel out thy heart : recover these,
And thou mayst offer many gifts in one.

There is a balsam, or indeed a blood,
Drooping from heaven, which doth both cleanse and
    close
All sorts of wounds ; of such strange force it is.
Seek out this All-heal, and seek no repose,
Until thou find, and use it to thy good :
Then bring thy gift ; and let thy hymn be this;

            SINCE my sadness
             Into gladness,
       Lord, Thou dost convert,
              O accept
            What Thou hast kept,
      As Thy due desert.

             Had I many,
              Had I any,
      (For this heart is none)
            All were Thine
           And none of mine,
    Surely Thine alone.

            Yet Thy favour
            May give savour
    To this poor oblation ;
          And it raise
        To be Thy praise,
  And be my salvation.

LONGING

WITH sick and famished eyes,
   With doubling knees and weary bones,
     To Thee my cries,
     To Thee my groans,
To Thee my sighs, my tears ascend :
          No end ?

     My throat, my soul is hoarse ;
My heart is withered like a ground
      Which Thou dost curse.
      My thoughts turn round,
And make me giddy ; Lord, I fall,
          Yet call.

     From Thee all pity flows.
Mothers are kind, because Thou art,
      And dost dispose
      To them a part :
Their infants, them ; and they suck Thee
          More free.

     Bowels of pity, hear !
Lord of my soul, love of my mind,
      Bow down Thine ear !
      Let not the wind
Scatter my words, and in the same
          Thy name !

     Look on my sorrows round !
Mark well my furnace ! O what flames,
      What heats abound !
      What griefs, what shames !
Consider, Lord ; Lord, bow Thine ear.
          And hear !

Lord Jesu, Thou didst bow
Thy dying Head upon the tree:
O be not now
More dead to me!
Lord, hear! " Shall He that made the ear
Not hear?"

Behold, Thy dust doth stir;
It moves, it creeps, it aims at Thee:
Wilt Thou defer
To succour me,
Thy pile of dust, wherein each crumb
Says, Come?

To Thee help appertains.
Hast Thou left all things to their course,
And laid the reins
Upon the horse?
Is all locked? hath a sinner's plea
No key?

Indeed the world's Thy book,
Where all things have their leaf assigned:
Yet a meek look
Hath interlined.
Thy board is full, yet humble guests
Find nests.

Thou tarriest, while I die,
And fall to nothing: Thou dost reign,
And rule on high,
While I remain
In bitter grief: yet am I styled
Thy child.

Lord, didst Thou leave Thy throne,
Not to relieve? how can it be,
That Thou art grown
Thus hard to me?
Were sin alive, good cause there were
To bear.

But now both sin is dead,
And all Thy promises live and bide.
That wants his head;
These speak and chide,
And in Thy bosom pour my tears,
As theirs.

Lord JESU, hear my heart,
Which hath been broken now so long,
That every part
Hath got a tongue!
Thy beggars grow; rid them away
To-day.

My love, my sweetness, hear!
By these Thy feet, at which my heart
Lies all the year,
Pluck out Thy dart
And heal my troubled breast which cries,
Which dies.

THE BAG

AWAY despair; my gracious Lord doth hear,
  Though winds and waves assault my keel,
He doth preserve it: He doth steer,
E'en when the boat seems most to reel.

Storms are the triumph of His art:
Well may He close His eyes, but not His heart.

Hast thou not heard, that my Lord JESUS died?
    Then let me tell thee a strange story.
    The God of power, as He did ride
    In His majestic robes of glory,
    Resolved to light; and so one day
He did descend, undressing all the way.

The stars His tire of light and rings obtained,
    The clouds His bow, the fire His spear,
    The sky His azure mantle gained.
    And when they asked, what He would wear;
    He smiled, and said as He did go,
He had new clothes a making here below.

When He was come, as travellers are wont,
    He did repair unto an inn.
    Both then and after, many a brunt
    He did endure to cancel sin:
    And having given the rest before,
Here He gave up His life to pay our score.

But as He was returning, there came one
    That ran upon Him with a spear.
    He who came hither all alone,
    Bringing nor man, nor arms, nor fear,
    Received the blow upon His side,
And straight He turned, and to His brethren cried,

If ye have any thing to send or write,
    (I have no bag, but here is room)
    Unto My Father's hands and sight
    (Believe Me) it shall safely come.

That I shall mind, what you impart;
Look, you may put it very near My heart.

Or if hereafter any of My friends
    Will use Me in this kind the door
    Shall still be open; what he sends
    I will present, and somewhat more,
    Not to his hurt. Sighs will convey
Any thing to Me. Hark despair, away!

THE JEWS

POOR nation, whose sweet sap, and juice
   Our scions have purloined, and left you dry:
Whose streams we got by the Apostles' sluice
And use in baptism, while ye pine and die:
Who by not keeping once, became a debtor;
    And now by keeping lose the letter:

    O that my prayers! mine, alas!
O that some Angel might a trumpet sound:
At which the Church falling upon her face
Should cry so loud, until the trump were drowned,
And by that cry of her dear Lord obtain,
    That your sweet sap might come again!

THE COLLAR

I STRUCK the board, and cried, no more;
              I will abroad.
What? shall I ever sigh and pine?
My lines and life are free; free as the road,
Loose as the wind, as large as store.

Shall I be still in suit?
Have I no harvest but a thorn
To let me blood, and not restore
What I have lost with cordial fruit?
Sure there was wine,
Before my sighs did dry it : there was corn,
Before my tears did drown it.
Is the year only lost to me?
Have I no bays to crown it?
No flowers, no garlands gay? all blasted?
All wasted?
Not so, my heart : but there is fruit,
And thou hast hands.
Recover all thy sigh-blown age
On double pleasures : leave thy cold dispute
Of what is fit, and not : forsake thy cage,
Thy rope of sands,
Which petty thoughts have made, and made to thee
Good cable, to enforce and draw,
And be thy law,
While thou didst wink and wouldst not see.
Away ; take heed :
I will abroad.
Call in thy death's-head there : tie up thy fears.
He that forbears
To suit and serve his need,
Deserves his load.
But as I raved and grew more fierce and wild
At every word,
Methought I heard one calling, "Child :"
And I replied, "My Lord!"

THE GLIMPSE

WHITHER away delight?
 Thou camest but now; wilt thou so soon depart,
  And give me up to night?
For many weeks of lingering pain and smart
But one half hour of comfort for my heart?

  Methinks delight should have
More skill in music, and keep better time.
  Wert thou a wind or wave,
They quickly go and come with lesser crime:
Flowers look about, and die not in their prime.

  Thy short abode and stay
Feeds not, but adds to the desire of meat.
  Lime begged of old (they say)
A neighbour spring to cool his inward heat;
Which by the spring's access grew much more great.

  In hope of thee my heart
Picked here and there a crumb, and would not die;
  But constant to his part,
When as my fears foretold this, did reply,
A slender thread a gentle guest will tie.

  Yet if the heart that wept
Must let thee go, return when it doth knock.
  Although thy heap be kept
For future times, the droppings of the stock
May oft break forth, and never break the lock.

L.

If I have more to spin,
The wheel shall go, so that thy stay be short.
    Thou knowest how grief and sin
Disturb the work.   O make me not their sport,
Who by thy coming may be made a court!

ASSURANCE

O SPITEFUL bitter thought!
   Bitterly spiteful thought! Couldst thou invent
So high a torture?   Is such poison bought?
Doubtless, but in the way of punishment,
    When wit contrives to meet with thee,
   ·No such rank poison can there be.

    Thou said'st but even now,
That all was not so fair as I conceived,
Betwixt my God and me; that I allow
And coin large hopes; but, that I was deceived:
    Either the league was broke, or near it;
    And, that I had great cause to fear it.

    And what to this? What more
Could poison, if it had a tongue, express?
What is thy aim? Wouldst thou unlock the door
To cold despairs, and gnawing pensiveness?
    Wouldst thou raise devils?   I see, I know,
    I writ thy purpose long ago.

    But I will to my Father,
Who heard thee say it.   O most gracious Lord,
If all the hope and comfort that I gather,
Were from myself, I had not half a word,
    Not half a letter to oppose
    What is objected by my foes.

But Thou art my desert;
And in this league, which now my foes invade,
Thou art not only to perform Thy part,
But also mine; as when the league was made,
 Thou didst at once Thyself indite,
 And hold my hand, while I did write.

  Wherefore if Thou canst fail,
Then can Thy truth and I: but while rocks stand,
And rivers stir, Thou canst not shrink or quail:
Yea, when both rocks and all things shall disband,
 Then shalt Thou be my rock and tower,
 And make their ruin praise Thy power.

  Now, foolish thought, go on,
Spin out thy thread, and make thereof a coat
To hide thy shame: for thou hast cast a bone,
Which bounds on thee, and will not down thy throat.
 What for itself love once began,
 Now love and truth will end in man.

THE CALL

COME, my Way, my Truth, my Life:
 Such a Way, as gives us breath:
Such a Truth, as ends all strife:
Such a Life, as killeth death.

Come, my Light, my Feast, my Strength:
Such a Light, as shows a feast:
Such a Feast, as mends in length:
Such a Strength, as makes his guest.

Come, my Joy, my Love, my Heart:
Such a Joy, as none can move:
Such a Love, as none can part:
Such a Heart, as joys in love.

CLASPING OF HANDS

LORD, Thou art mine, and I am Thine,
If mine I am: and Thine much more,
Than I or ought, or can be mine.
Yet to be Thine, doth me restore;
So that again I now am mine,
And with advantage mine the more.
Since this being mine, brings with it Thine,
And Thou with me dost Thee restore.
    If I without Thee would be mine,
    I neither should be mine nor Thine.

Lord, I am Thine, and Thou art mine:
So mine Thou art, that something more
I may presume Thee mine, than Thine.
For Thou didst suffer to restore
Not Thee, but me, and to be mine:
And with advantage mine the more,
Since Thou in death wast none of Thine,
Yet then as mine didst me restore.
    O be mine still! still make me Thine
    Or rather make no Thine and Mine!

PRAISE

LORD, I will mean and speak Thy praise,
          Thy praise alone.
My busy heart shall spin it all my days:
    And when it stops for want of store,
Then will I wring it with a sigh or groan,
          That Thou mayst yet have more.

When Thou dost favour any action,
          It runs, it flies:
All things concur to give it a perfection.
    That which had but two legs before,   [rise
When Thou dost bless, hath twelve: one wheel doth
          To twenty then, or more.

But when Thou dost on business blow,
          It hangs, it clogs:
Not all the teams of Albion in a row
    Can hale or draw it out of door.
Legs are but stumps, and Pharaoh's wheels but logs,
          And struggling hinders more.

Thousands of things do thee employ
          In ruling all
This spacious globe. Angels must have their joy,
    Devils their rod, the sea his shore,
The winds their stint: and yet when I did call,
          Thou heard'st my call, and more.

I have not lost one single tear:
          But when mine eyes
Did weep to heaven, they found a bottle there
    (As we have boxes for the poor)

Ready to to take them in ; yet of a size
    That would contain much more.

But after Thou hadst slipt a drop
    From Thy right eye
(Which there did hang like streamers near the top
    Of some fair church, to show the sore ,
And bloody battle which Thou once didst try)
    The glass was full and more.

Wherefore I sing.   Yet since my heart,
    Though pressed, runs thin ;
O that I might some other hearts convert,
    And so take up at use good store :
That to Thy chests there might be coming in
    Both all my praise, and more !

JOSEPH'S COAT

WOUNDED I sing, tormented I endite,
    Thrown down I fall into a bed, and rest :
Sorrow hath changed its note : such is His will
Who changeth all things, as Him pleaseth best.
    For well He knows, if but one grief and smart
Among my many had his full career,
Sure it would carry with it e'en my heart,
And both would run until they found a bier
    To fetch the body ; both being due to grief.
But He hath spoiled the race ; and given to anguish
One of joy's coats, 'ticing it with relief
To linger in me, and together languish.
    I live to show His power, Who once did bring
    My joys to weep, and now my griefs to sing.

THE PULLEY

WHEN God at first made man,
  Having a glass of blessing standing by;
Let us (said He) pour on him all we can:
Let the world's riches, which dispersed lie,
  Contract into a span.

So strength first made a way;
Then beauty flowed, then wisdom, honour, pleasure:
When almost all was out, God made a stay,
Perceiving that alone of all His treasure,
  Rest, in the bottom lay.

For if I should (said He)
Bestow this jewel also on My creature,
He would adore My gifts instead of Me,
And rest in nature, not the God of nature:
  So both should losers be.

Yet let him keep the rest,
But keep them with repining restlessness:
Let him be rich and weary, that at least,
If goodness lead him not, yet weariness
  May toss him to My breast.

THE PRIESTHOOD

BLEST Order, which in power doth so excel,
  That with the one hand thou liftest to the sky,
And with the other throwest down to hell
In thy just censures; fain would I draw nigh;
Fain put thee on. exchanging my lay sword
      For that of the Holy Word.

But thou art fire, sacred and hallowed fire;
And I but earth and clay: should I presume
To wear thy habit, the severe attire
My slender compositions might consume.
I am both foul and brittle, much unfit
           To deal in Holy Writ.

Yet have I often seen, by cunning hand
And force of fire, what curious things are made
Of wretched earth.   Where once I scorned to stand,
That earth is fitted by the fire and trade
Of skilful artists, for the boards of those
           Who make the bravest shows.

But since those great ones, be they ne'er so great,
Come from the earth, from whence those vessels come;
So that at once both feeder, dish, and meat,
Have one beginning and one final sum:
I do not greatly wonder at the sight,
           If earth in earth delight.

But the holy men of God such vessels are,
As serve Him up, Who all the world commands.
When God vouchsafeth to become our fare,
Their hands convey Him, Who conveys their hands:
O what pure things, most pure must those things be,
           Who bring my God to me!

Wherefore I dare not, I, put forth my hand
To hold the Ark, although it seem to shake
Through the old sins and new doctrines of our land.
Only, since God doth often vessels make
Of lowly matter for high uses meet,
           I throw me at His feet.

There will I lie, until my Maker seek
For some mean stuff whereon to shew His skill:
Then is my time. The distance of the meek
Doth flatter power. Lest good come short of ill
In praising might, the poor do by submission
          What pride by opposition.

THE SEARCH

WHITHER, O, whither art Thou fled,
        My Lord, my Love?
My searches are my daily bread;
        Yet never prove.

My knees pierce the earth, mine eyes the sky:
        And yet the sphere
And centre both to me deny
        That Thou art there.

Yet can I mark how herbs below
        Grow green and gay;
As if to meet Thee they did know,
        While I decay.

Yet can I mark how stars above
        Simper and shine,
As having keys unto Thy love,
        While poor I pine.

I sent a sigh to seek Thee out,
        Deep drawn in pain,
Winged like an arrow: but my scout
        Returns in vain.

I turned another (having store)
        Into a groan,
Because the search was dumb before:
        But all was one.

Lord, dost Thou some new fabric mould
        Which favour wins,
And keeps Thee present, leaving the old
        Unto their sins?

Where is my God? what hidden place
        Conceals Thee still?
What covert dare eclipse Thy face?
        Is it Thy will?

O let not that of anything:
        Let rather brass,
Or steel, or mountains be Thy ring.
        And I will pass.

Thy will such an intrenching is,
        As passeth thought:
To it all strength, all subtilties
        Are things of nought.

Thy will such a strange distance is,
        As that to it
East and West touch, the poles do kiss,
        And parallels meet.

Since then my grief must be as large
        As is Thy space,
Thy distance from me; see my charge,
        Lord, see my case.

O take these bars, these lengths, away;
　　　　Turn, and restore me:
Be not Almighty, let me say,
　　　　Against, but for me.

When Thou dost turn, and wilt be near;
　　　　What edge so keen,
What point so piercing can appear
　　　　To come between?

For as Thy absence doth excel
　　　　All distance known:
So doth Thy nearness bear the bell,
　　　　Making two one.

GRIEF

O WHO will give me tears? Come all ye springs,
　Dwell in my head and eyes: come, clouds, and
　　rain:
My grief hath need of all the watery things,
That nature hath produced.　Let every vein
Suck up a river to supply mine eyes,
My weary weeping eyes to dry for me,
Unless they get new conduits, new supplies,
To bear them out, and with my state agree.
What are two shallow fords, two little spouts,
Of a less world? the greater is but small,
A narrow cupboard for my griefs and doubts,
Which want provision in the midst of all.
Verses, ye are too fine a thing, too wise
For my rough sorrows: cease, be dumb and mute,
Give up your feet and running to mine eyes,

And keep your measures for some lover's lute,
Whose grief allows him music and a rhyme :
For mine excludes both measure, tune, and time.
         Alas, my God !

THE CROSS

WHAT is this strange and uncouth thing
       To make me sigh, and seek, and faint, and
          die,
Until I had some place, where I might sing,
       And serve Thee ; and not only I,   ·
But all my wealth, and family might combine
To set Thy honour up, as our design.

And then, when after much delay,
Much wrestling, many a combat, this dear end,
So much desired, is given, to take away
       My power to serve Thee : to unbend
All my abilities, my designs confound,
And lay my threatenings bleeding on the ground.

One ague dwelleth in my bones,
Another in my soul (the memory
What I would do for Thee, if once my groans
       Could be allowed for harmony)
I am in all a weak disabled thing,
Save in the sight thereof, where strength doth sting,

Besides, things sort not to my will,
E'en when my will doth study Thy renown :
Thou turnest the edge of all things on me still,
       Taking me up to throw me down :
So that, e'en when my hopes seem to be sped,
I am to grief alive, to them as dead.

To have my aim, and yet to be
Farther from it than when I bent my bow ;
To make my hopes the torture, and the fee
    Of all my woes another woe,
Is in the midst of delicates to need,
And e'en in Paradise to be a weed.

    Ah, my dear Father, ease my smart !
These contrarieties crush me : these cross actions
Do wind a rope about, and cut my heart :
    And yet since these Thy contradictions
Are properly a cross felt by Thy Son,
With but four words, my words, " Thy will be done."

THE FLOWER

HOW fresh, O Lord, how sweet and clean
   Are Thy returns ! e'en as the flowers in spring ;
    To which, besides their own demean,
The late-past frosts tributes of pleasure bring.
        Grief melts away
        Like snow in May,
As if there were no such cold thing.

    Who would have thought my shrivelled heart
Could have recovered greenness ? It was gone
    Quite under ground ; as flowers depart
To see their mother-root, when they have blown ;
        Where they together
        All the hard weather,
Dead to the world, keep house unknown.

These are Thy wonders, Lord of power,
Killing and quickening, bringing down to hell
    And up to heaven in an hour :
Making a chiming of a passing bell.
        We say amiss,
        This or that is :
Thy word is all, if we could spell.

O that I once past changing were,
Fast in Thy Paradise, where no flower can wither !
    Many a spring I shoot up fair,
Offering at heaven, growing and groaning thither :
        Nor doth my flower
        Want a spring-shower,
My sins and I joining together.

But while I grow in a straight line,
Still upwards bent, as if heaven were mine own,
    Thy anger comes, and I decline :
What frost to that? what pole is not the zone
        Where all things burn,
        When Thou dost turn,
And the least frown of Thine is shown?

And now in age I bud again,
After so many deaths I live and write ;
    I once more smell the dew and rain,
And relish versing : O my only Light,
        It cannot be
        That I am he,
On whom Thy tempests fell at night.

These are Thy wonders, Lord of love.
To make us see we are but flowers that glide :

Which when we once can find and prove,
Thou hast a garden for us, where to bide.
Who would be more,
Swelling through store,
Forfeit their Paradise by pride.

DOTAGE

FALSE glozing pleasures, casks of happiness,
    Foolish night-fires, women's and children's
        wishes,
Chases in arras, gilded emptiness,
Shadows well mounted, dreams in a career,
Embroidered lies, nothing between two dishes;
        These are the pleasures here.

True earnest sorrows, rooted miseries,
Anguish in grain, vexations ripe and blown,
Sure-footed griefs, solid calamities,
Plain demonstrations, evident and clear,
Fetching their proofs e'en from the very bone;
        These are the sorrows here.

But O the folly of distracted men,
Who griefs in earnest, joys in jest pursue;
Preferring, like brute beasts, a loathsome den
Before a court, e'en that above so clear,
Where are no sorrows, but delights more true
        Than miseries are here!

THE SON

LET foreign Nations of their language boast,
'What fine variety each tongue affords :
I like our language, as our men and coast;
Who cannot dress it well, want wit, not words.
How neatly do we give one only name
To parents issue and the sun's bright star!
A son is light and fruit : a fruitful flame
Chasing the father's dimness, carried far
From the first man in the east, to fresh and new
Western discoveries of posterity.
So in one word our Lord's humility
We turn upon Him in a sense most true :
    For what Christ once in humbleness began,
    We Him in glory call, " The Son of man."

A TRUE HYMN

MY joy, my life, my crown!
    My heart was meaning all the day,
      Somewhat it fain would say :
And still it runneth muttering up and down
With only this, " My joy, my life, my crown !"

      Yet slight not these few words;
    If truly said, they may take part
      Among the best in art.
The fineness which a hymn or psalm affords,
Is, when the soul unto the lines accords.

He who craves all the mind,
And all the soul, and strength, and time,
If the words only rhyme,
Justly complains, that somewhat is behind
To make his verse, or write a hymn in kind.

Whereas if the heart be moved,
Although the verse be somewhat scant,
God doth supply the want:
As when the heart says (sighing to be approved)
" O, could I love!" and stops; God writeth, "Loved."

THE ANSWER

MY comforts drop and melt away like snow:
I shake my head, and all the thoughts and ends,
Which my fierce youth did bandy, fall and flow
Like leaves about me, or like summer friends,
Flies of estates and sunshine. But to all,
Who think me eager, hot, and undertaking,
But in my prosecutions slack and small;
As a young exhalation, newly waking,
Scorns his first bed of dirt, and means the sky;
But cooling by the way, grows pursy and slow,
And settling to a cloud, doth live and die
In that dark state of tears; to all, that so
Show me, and set me, I have one reply,
Which they that know the rest, know more than I.

A DIALOGUE-ANTHEM

CHRISTIAN, DEATH.

Chr.　ALAS, poor death! where is thy glory?
　　　Where is thy famous force, thy ancient
　　　　sting?

Dea.　Alas, poor mortal, void of story,
　　　Go spell and read how I have killed thy King.

Chr.　Poor death! and who was hurt thereby?
　　　Thy curse being laid on Him mak'st thee accurst.

Dea.　Let losers talk, yet thou shalt die;
　　　These arms shall crush thee.
Chr.　　　　　　　　　　Spare not, do thy worst.
　　　I shall be one day better than before:
　　　Thou so much worse, that thou shalt be no more.

THE WATER-COURSE

THOU who dost dwell and linger here below,
　Since the condition of this world is frail,
Where of all plants afflictions soonest grow;
If troubles overtake thee, do not wail:
　For who can look for less that loveth $\left\{ \begin{array}{l} \text{Life.} \\ \text{Strife.} \end{array} \right.$

But rather turn the pipe, and water's course
To serve thy sins, and furnish thee with store
Of sovereign tears, springing from true remorse:
That so in pureness thou mayst Him adore
　Who gives to man, as He sees fit, $\left\{ \begin{array}{l} \text{Salvation.} \\ \text{Damnation.} \end{array} \right.$

SELF-CONDEMNATION

THOU who condemnest Jewish hate,
   For choosing Barabbas a murderer
         Before the Lord of glory;
   Look back upon thine own estate,
Call home thine eye (that busy wanderer)
         That choice may be thy story.

   He that doth love, and love amiss
This world's delights before true Christian joy, .
         Hath made a Jewish choice:
   The world an ancient murderer is;
Thousands of souls it hath and doth destroy
         With her enchanting voice.

   He that hath made a sorry wedding
Between his soul and gold, and hath preferred
         False gain before the true.
   Hath done what he condemns in reading:
For he hath sold for money his dear Lord
         And is a Judas-Jew.

   Thus we prevent the last great day,
And judge ourselves. That light which sin and passion
         Did before dim and choke,
   When once those snuffs are ta'en away,
Shines bright and clear, e'en unto condemnation,
         Without excuse or cloak.

BITTER-SWEET

AH, my dear angry Lord,
   Since Thou dost love, yet strike;
Cast down, yet help afford;
   Sure I will do the like.

I will complain, yet praise;
I will bewail, approve:
And all my sour-sweet days
I will lament, and love.

THE GLANCE

WHEN first Thy sweet and gracious eye
   Vouchsafed e'en in the midst of youth and night
To look upon me, who before did lie
     Weltering in sin;
   I felt a sugared strange delight,
Passing all cordials made by any art,
Bedew, embalm, and overrun my heart,
     And take it in.

     Since that time many a bitter storm
My soul hath felt, e'en able to destroy,
Had the malicious and ill-meaning harm
     His swing and sway:
   But still Thy sweet original joy,
Sprung from Thine eye, did work within my soul,
And surging griefs, when they grew bold, control,
     And got the day.

If Thy first glance so powerful be,
A mirth but opened, and sealed up again ;
What wonders shall we feel, when we shall see
Thy full-eyed love!
When Thou shalt look us out of pain,
And one aspect of Thine spend in delight
More than a thousand suns disburse in light,
In Heaven above.

THE TWENTY-THIRD PSALM

THE God of love my Shepherd is,
And He that doth me feed :
While He is mine, and I am His,
What can I want or need?

He leads me to the tender grass,
Where I both feed and rest;
Then to the streams that gently pass;
In both I have the best.

Or if I stray, He doth convert,
And bring my mind in frame :
And all this not for my desert,
But for His holy name.

Yea, in death's shady black abode
Well may I walk, not fear:
For Thou art with me, and Thy rod
To guide, Thy staff to bear.

Nay, Thou dost make me sit and dine,
　　E'en in my enemies' sight;
My head with oil, my cup with wine
　　Runs over day and night.

Surely Thy sweet and wondrous love
　　Shall measure all my days;
And as it never shall remove,
　　So neither shall my praise.

MARY MAGDALEN

WHEN blessed Mary wiped her Saviour's feet,
　　(Whose precepts she had trampled on before)
And wore them for a jewel on her head,
　　Showing His steps should be the street,
　　Wherein she thenceforth evermore
With pensive humbleness would live and tread:

She being stained herself, why did she strive
To make Him clean, Who could not be defiled:
Why kept she not her tears for her own faults,
　　And not His feet?　Though we could dive
　　In tears like seas, our sins are piled
Deeper than they, in words, and works, and thoughts.

Dear soul, she knew Who did vouchsafe and deign
To bear her filth: and that her sins did dash
E'en God Himself: wherefore she was not loath,
　　As she had brought wherewith to stain,
　　So to bring in wherewith to wash:
And yet in washing one, she washed both.

AARON

H OLINESS on the head,
    Light and perfections on the breast,
Harmonious bells below, raising the dead
  To lead them unto life and rest.
    Thus are true Aarons drest.

    Profaneness in my head,
  Defects and darkness in my breast,
A noise of passions ringing me for dead
  Unto a place where is no rest:
    Poor Priest! thus am I drest.

    Only another head
  I have, another heart and breast,
Another music, making live, not dead,
  Without Whom I could have no rest:
    In Him I am well drest.

    Christ is my only head,
  My alone only heart and breast,
My only music, striking me e'en dead;
  That to the old man I may rest,
    And be in Him new drest.

    So holy in my head,
  Perfect and light in my dear breast,
My doctrine tuned by Christ, (who is not dead;
  But lives in me while I do rest)
    Come, people; Aaron's drest.

THE ODOUR

2 Cor. ii. 15.

HOW sweetly doth My Master sound! My Master!
   As ambergris leaves a rich scent
      Unto the taster:
   So do these words a sweet content,
An oriental fragrancy, My Master.

With these all day I do perfume my mind,
   My mind e'en thrust into them both;
      That I might find
   What cordials make this curious broth,
This broth of smells that feeds and fats my mind.

My Master, shall I speak?   O that to Thee
   My Servant were a little so,
      As flesh may be;
   That these two words might creep and grow
To some degree of spiciness to Thee!

Then should the pomander, which was before
   A speaking sweet, mend by reflection,
      And tell me more:
   For pardon of my imperfection
Would warm and work it sweeter than before.

For when My Master, which alone is sweet,
   And e'en in my unworthiness pleasing,
      Shall call and meet,
   My Servant, as Thee not displeasing,
That call is but the breathing of the sweet.

This breathing would with gains by sweetening me
(As sweet things traffic when they meet)
    Return to Thee,
And so this new commerce and sweet
Should all my life employ, and busy me.

THE FOIL

IF we could see below
    The sphere of virtue, and each shining grace
        As plainly as that above doth show;
This were the better sky, the brighter place.

    God hath made stars the foil
To set off virtues; griefs to set off sinning.
    Yet in this wretched world we toil,
As if grief were not foul, nor virtue winning.

THE FORERUNNERS

THE harbingers are come. See, see their mark;
    White is their colour, and behold my head.
But must they have my brain? must they dispark
Those sparkling notions, which therein were bred?
    Must dulness turn me to a clod?
Yet have they left me, "Thou art still my God."

Good men ye be, to leave me my best room,
E'en all my heart, and what is lodged there:
I pass not, I what of the rest become,
So, "Thou art still my God," be out of fear.
    He will be pleased with that ditty;
And if I please Him, I write fine and witty.

Farewell sweet phrases, lovely metaphors:
But will ye leave me thus? when ye before
Of stews and brothels only knew the doors,
Then did I wash you with my tears, and more,
    Brought you to church well drest and clad:
My God must have my best, e'en all I had.

Lovely enchanting language, sugarcane,
Honey of roses, whither wilt thou fly?
Hath some fond lover 'ticed thee to thy bane?
And wilt thou leave the church, and love a sty?
    Fie, thou wilt soil thy broider'd coat,
And hurt thyself, and him that sings the note.

Let foolish lovers, if they will love dung,
With canvas, not with arras clothe their shame:
Let folly speak in her own native tongue.
True beauty dwells on high: ours is a flame
    But borrowed thence to light us thither.
Beauty and beauteous words should go together.

Yet if you go, I pass not; take your way:
For, "Thou art still my God," is all that ye
Perhaps with more embellishment can say.
Go, birds of spring: let winter have his fee;
    Let a bleak paleness chalk the door,
So all within be livelier than before.

THE ROSE

PRESS me not to take more pleasure
    In this world of sugar'd lies,
And to use a larger measure
    Than my strict, yet welcome size.

First, there is no pleasure here:
    Coloured griefs indeed there are,
Blushing woes, that look as clear,   .
    As if they could beauty spare.

Or if such deceits there be,
    Such delights I meant to say;
There are no such things to me,
    Who have passed my right away.

But I will not much oppose
    Unto what you now advise:
Only take this gentle rose,
    And therein my answer lies.

What is fairer than a rose?
    What is sweeter? yet it purgeth.
Purgings enmity disclose,
    Enmity forbearance urgeth.

If then all that worldlings prize
    Be contracted to a rose;
Sweetly there indeed it lies,
    But it biteth in the close.

So this flower doth judge and sentence
    Worldly joys to be a scourge;
For they all produce repentance,
    And repentance is a purge.

But I health, not physic, choose:
    Only though I you oppose,
Say that fairly I refuse,
    For my answer is a rose.

DISCIPLINE

THROW away Thy rod,
   Throw away Thy wrath:
      O my God,
Take the gentle path.

For my heart's desire
Unto Thine is bent:
      I aspire
To a full consent.

Not a word or look
I affect to own,
      But by book,
And Thy book alone.

Though I fail, I weep:
Though I halt in pace,
      Yet I creep
To the throne of grace.

Then let wrath remove;
Love will do the deed:
      For with love
Stony hearts will bleed

Love is swift of foot;
Love's a man of war,
      And can shoot,
And can hit from far.

Who can 'scape his bow?
That which wrought on Thee,
    Brought Thee low,
Needs must work on me.

Throw away Thy rod;
Though man frailties hath,
    Thou art God:
Throw away Thy wrath.

THE INVITATION

COME ye hither, all whose taste
    Is your waste;
Save your cost, and mend your fare.
God is here prepared and dressed,
    And the feast,
God, in whom all dainties are.

Come ye hither, all whom wine
    Doth define,
Naming you not to your good:
Weep what ye have drunk amiss,
    And drink this,
Which before ye drink is blood.

Come ye hither, all whom pain
    Doth arraign,
Bringing all your sins to sight:
Taste and fear not: God is here
    In this cheer,
And on sin doth cast the fright.

Come ye hither, all whom joy
        Doth destroy,
While ye graze without your bounds:
Here is joy that drowneth quite
        Your delight,
As a flood the lower grounds.

Come ye hither, all whose love
        Is your dove,
And exalts you to the sky:
Here is love, which, having breath
        E'en in death,
After death can never die.

Lord, I have invited all,
        And I shall
Still invite, still call to Thee:
For it seems but just and right
        In my sight,
Where is all, there all should be.

THE BANQUET

WELCOME sweet and sacred cheer,
        Welcome dear;
With me, in me, live and dwell:
For thy neatness passeth sight,
        Thy delight
Passeth tongue to taste or tell.

O what sweetness from the bowl
        Fills my soul,

Such as is, and makes divine!
Is some star (fled from the sphere)
                    Melted there,
As we sugar melt in wine?

Or hath sweetness in the bread
                    Made a head
To subdue the smell of sin,
Flowers, and gums, and powders giving
                    All their living,
Lest the enemy should win?

Doubtless neither star nor flower
                    Hath the power
Such a sweetness to impart:
Only God, who gives perfumes,
                    Flesh assumes,
And with it perfumes my heart.

But as pomanders and wood
                    Still are good,
Yet being bruised are better scented;
God, to show how far His love
                    Could improve,
Here, as broken, is presented.

When I had forgot my birth,
                    And on earth
In delights of earth was drowned;
God took blood, and needs would be
                    Spilt with me,
And so found me on the ground.

Having raised me to look up,
In a cup
Sweetly He doth meet my taste;
But I still being low and short,
Far from court,
Wine becomes a wing at last.

For with it alone I fly
To the sky:
Where I wipe mine eyes, and see
What I'seek, for what I sue;
Him I view
Who hath done so much for me.

Let the wonder of this pity
Be my ditty,
And take up my lines and life:
Hearken unto pain of death,
Hands and breath,
Strive in this, and love the strife.

THE POSY

LET wits contest,
And with their words and posies windows fill:
"Less than the least
Of all Thy mercies," is my posy still.

This on my ring,
This by my picture, in my book I write;
Whether I sing,
Or say, or dictate, this is my delight.

Invention rest;
Comparisons go play; wit use thy will:
"Less than the least
Of all God's mercies," is my posy still.

A PARODY

SOUL'S joy, when Thou art gone,
    And I alone,
    Which cannot be,
Because Thou dost abide with me,
    And I depend on Thee;

Yet when Thou dost suppress
    The cheerfulness
    Of Thy abode,
And in my powers not stir abroad,
    But leave me to my load:

O what a damp and shade
    Doth me invade!
    No stormy night
Can so afflict or so affright
    As Thy eclipsed light.

Ah Lord! do not withdraw,
    Lest want of awe
    Make sin appear;
And when Thou dost but shine less clear,
    Say, that Thou art not here.

And then what life I have,
     While sin doth rave,
     And falsely boast,
That I may seek, but Thou art lost!
     Thou and alone Thou knowest.

O what a deadly cold
     Doth me infold!
     I half believe,
That sin says true: but while I grieve,
     Thou comest and dost relieve.

THE ELIXIR

TEACH me, my God and King,
     In all things Thee to see,
And what I do in anything,
     To do it as for Thee:

Not rudely, as a beast,
     To run into an action;
But still to make Thee prepossest,
     And give it his perfection.

A man that looks on glass,
     On it may stay his eye;
Or if he pleaseth, through it pass,
     And then the heaven espy.

All may of Thee partake:
     Nothing can be so mean,
Which with this tincture "for Thy sake"
     Will not grow bright and clean.

A servant with this clause
Makes drudgery divine:
Who sweeps a room, as for Thy laws,
Makes that and the action fine.

This is the famous stone
That turneth all to gold:
For that which God doth touch and own
Cannot for less be told.

A WREATH

A WREATHED garland of deserved praise,
Of praise deserved, unto Thee I give, .
I give to Thee, who knowest all my ways,
My crooked winding ways, wherein I live,
Wherein I die, not live; for life is straight,
Straight as a line, and ever tends to Thee,
To Thee, who art more far above deceit,
Than deceit seems above simplicity.
Give me simplicity, that I may live,
So live and like, that I may know Thy ways,
Know them and practise them: then shall I give
For this poor wreath, give Thee a crown of praise.

DEATH

DEATH, thou wast once an uncouth hideous thing,
Nothing but bones,
The sad effect of sadder groans:
Thy mouth was open, but thou couldst not sing.

For we considered thee as at some six
         Or ten years hence,
    After the loss of life and sense,
Flesh being turned to dust, and bones to sticks.

We looked on this side of thee, shooting short ;
        Where we did find
    The shells of fledge souls left behind,
Dry dust, which sheds no tears, but may extort.

But since our Savionr's death did put some blood
        Into thy face :
    Thou art grown fair and full of grace,
Much in request, much sought for, as a good.

For we do now behold thee gay and glad,
        As at doomsday;
    When souls shall wear their new array.
And all thy bones with beauty shall be clad.

Therefore we can go die as sleep, and trust
        Half that we have
    Unto an honest faithful grave ;
Making our pillows either down or dust.

DOOMSDAY

COME away.
      Make no delay.
Summon all the dust to rise,
Till it stir, and rub the eyes ;
While this member jogs the other,
Each one whispering, " Live you, Brother?"

Come away,
Make this the day.
Dust, alas, no music feels,
But thy trumpet: then it kneels,
As peculiar notes and strains ·
Cure tarantula's raging pains.

Come away,
O make no stay!
Let the graves make their confession,
Lest at length they plead possession:
Flesh's stubbornness may have
Read that lesson to the grave.

Come away,
Thy flock doth stray,
Some to the winds their body lend,
And in them may drown a friend:
Some in noisome vapours grow
To a plague and public woe.

Come away,
Help our decay.
Man is out of order hurled,
Parcelled out to all the world.
Lord, Thy broken concert_raise,
And the music shall be praise.

JUDGEMENT

ALMIGHTY Judge, how shall poor wretches
      Thy dreadful look,   [brook
   Able a heart of iron to appal,
     When Thou shalt call
  For every man's peculiar book?

What others mean to do, I know not well;
Yet I hear tell,
That some will turn Thee to some leaves therein
So void of sin,
That they in merit shall excel.

But I resolve, when Thou shalt call for mine,
That to decline,
And thrust a Testament into Thy hand:
Let that be scanned.
There Thou shalt find my faults are Thine.

HEAVEN

O WHO will show me those delights on high?
    Echo.   *I.*
Thou, Echo? thou art mortal, all men know.
    Echo.   *No.*
Wert thou not born among the trees and leaves?
    Echo.   *Leaves.*
And are there any leaves, that still abide?
    Echo.   *Bide.*
What leaves are they? impart the matter wholly.
    Echo.   *Holy.*
Are holy leaves the echo then of bliss?
    Echo.   *Yes.*
Then tell me, what is that supreme delight?
    Echo.   *Light.*
Light to the mind: what shall the will enjoy?
    Echo.   *Joy.*
But are there cares and business with the pleasure?
    Echo.   *Leisure.*
Light, joy, and leisure; but shall they persevere?
    Echo.   *Ever.*

LOVE

LOVE bade me welcome : yet my soul drew back,
      Guilty of dust and sin.
But quick-eyed Love, observing me grow slack
      From my first entrance in,
Drew nearer to me, sweetly questioning,
      If I lacked anything.

A guest, I answered, worthy to be here :
      Love said, You shall be he.
I the unkind, ungrateful ? Ah my dear,
      I cannot look on thee.
Love took my hand, and smiling did reply,
      Who made the eyes but I ?

Truth, Lord, but I have marred them : let my shame
      Go where it doth deserve.
And know you not, says Love, who bore the blame ?
      My dear, then I will serve.
You must sit down, says Love, and taste my meat :
      So I did sit and eat.

*Glory be to God on high, and on earth peace, good
    will towards men.*

The Church Militant

THE CHURCH MILITANT

ALMIGHTY Lord, who from Thy glorious throne
    Seest and rulest all things e'en as one:
The smallest ant or atom knows Thy power,
Known also to each minute of an hour:
Much more do common-weals acknowledge Thee,
And wrap their policies in Thy decree,
Complying with Thy counsels, doing nought
Which doth not meet with an eternal thought.
But above all, Thy Church and Spouse doth prove
Not the decrees of power, but bands of love.
Early didst Thou arise to plant this Vine,
Which might the more endear it to be Thine.
Spices come from the East; so did Thy Spouse,
Trim as the light, sweet as the laden boughs
Of Noah's shady vine, chaste as the dove,
Prepared and fitted to receive Thy love.
The course was westward, that the sun might light
As well our understanding as our sight.
Where the ark did rest, there Abraham began
To bring the other ark from Canaan.
Moses pursued this: but king Solomon
Finished and fixed the old religion.
When it grew loose, the Jews did hope in vain
By nailing Christ to fasten it again;
But to the Gentiles He bore cross and all,
Rending with earthquakes the partition-wall.
Only whereas the ark in glory shone,
Now with the cross, as with a staff, alone,

Religion, like a pilgrim, westward bent,
Knocking at all doors, ever as she went.
Yet as the sun, though forward be his flight,
Listens behind him, and allows some light,
Till all depart : so went the Church her way,
Letting, while one foot stept, the other stay
Among the eastern nations for a time,
Till both removed to the western clime.
To Egypt first she came, where they did prove
Wonders of anger once, but now of love.
The ten commandments there did flourish more
Than the ten bitter plagues had done before.
Holy Macarius and great Anthony
Made Pharaoh Moses, changing the history.
Goshen was darkness, Egypt full of lights,
Nilus for monsters brought forth Israelites.
Such power hath mighty Baptism to produce,
For things misshapen, things of highest use.
"How dear to me, O God, Thy counsels are !
                 Who may with Thee compare?"
Religion thence fled into Greece, where arts
Gave her the highest place in all men's hearts.
Learning was posed, philosophy was set,
Sophisters taken in a fisher's net.
Plato and Aristotle were at a loss,
And wheeled about again to spell Christ's-cross.
Prayers chased syllogisms into their den,
And "Ergo" was transformed into "Amen."
Though Greece took horse as soon as Egypt did,
And Rome as both; yet Egypt faster rid,
And spent her period and prefixed time
Before the other. Greece being past her prime,
Religion went to Rome, subduing those,
Who, that they might subdue, made all their foes.
The warrior his dear scars no more resounds,
But seems to yield Christ hath the greater wounds;

Wounds willingly endured to work his bliss,
Who by an ambush lost his Paradise.
The great heart stoops, and taketh from the dust
A sad repentance, not the spoils of lust:
Quitting his spear lest it should pierce again
Him in His members, Who for him was slain.
The shepherd's hook grew to a sceptre here,
Giving new names and numbers to the year.
But the empire dwelt in Greece, to comfort them,
Who were cut short in Alexander's stem.
In both of these prowess and arts did tame
And tune men's hearts against the Gospel came:
Which using, and not fearing skill in the one,
Or strength in the other, did erect her throne,
Many a rent and struggling the empire knew,
(As dying things are wont,) until it flew
At length to Germany, still westward bending,
And there the Church's festival attending:
That as before empire and arts made way,
(For no less harbingers would serve than they)
So they might still, and point us out the place,
Where first the Church should raise her downcast face.
Strength levels grounds, art makes a garden there;
Then showers Religion, and makes all to bear.
Spain in the empire shared with Germany,
But England in the higher victory;
Giving the Church a crown to keep her state,
And not go less than she had done of late.
Constantine's British line meant this of old,
And did this mystery wrap up and fold
Within a sheet of paper, which was rent
From time's great chronicle, and hither sent.
Thus both the Church and sun together ran
Unto the farthest old meridian.
"How dear to me, O God, Thy counsels are!
          Who may with Thee compare?"

Much about one and the same time and place,
Both where and when the Church began her race,
Sin did set out of eastern Babylon,
And travelled westward also: journeying on
He chid the Church away, where'er he came,
Breaking her peace, and tainting her good name.
At first he got to Egypt, and did sow
Gardens of gods, which every year did grow
Fresh and fine deities.   They were at great cost,
Who for a god clearly a sallet lost.
Ah, what a thing is man devoid of grace,
Adoring garlic with an humble face,
Begging his food of that which he may eat,
Starving the while he worshippeth his meat!
Who makes a root his god, how low is he,
If God and man be served infinitely!
What wretchedness can give him any-room,
Whose house is foul, while he adores his broom?
None will believe this now, though money be
In us the same transplanted foolery.
Thus sin in Egypt sneaked for a while;
His highest was an ox or crocodile,
And such poor game.   Thence he to Greece doth pass,
And being craftier much than goodness was,
He left behind him garrisons of sins,
To make good that which every day he wins.
Here sin took heart, and for a garden-bed
Rich shrines and oracles he purchased:
He grew a gallant, and would needs foretell
As well what should befall, as what befell.
Nay, he became a poet, and would serve
His pills of sublimate in that conserve.
The world came both with hands and purses full
To this great lottery, and all would pull.
But all was glorious cheating, brave deceit,
Where some poor truths were shuffled for a bait

To credit him, and to discredit those,
Who after him should braver truths disclose.
From Greece he went to Rome: and as before
He was a god, now he's an emperor.
Nero and others lodged him bravely there,
Put him in trust to rule the Roman sphere.
Glory was his chief instrument of old:
Pleasure succeeded straight, when that grew cold:
Which soon was blown to such a mighty flame,
That though our Saviour did destroy the game,
Disparking oracles, and all their treasure,
Setting affliction to encounter pleasure;
Yet did a rogue with hope of carnal joy,
Cheat the most subtle nations.   Who so coy,
So trim, as Greece and Egypt? yet their hearts
Are given over, for their curious arts,
To such Mahometan stupidities,
As the old Heathen would deem prodigies.
" How dear to me, O God, Thy counsels are!
                    Who may with Thee compare? "
Only the West and Rome do keep them free
From this contagious infidelity.
And this is all the rock, whereof they boast,
As Rome will one day find unto her cost.
Sin being not able to extirpate quite
The Churches here, bravely resolved one night
To be a Churchman too, and wear a mitre:
The old debauched ruffian would turn writer.
I saw him in his study, where he sate
Busy in controversies sprung of late.
A gown and pen became him wondrous well:
His grave aspect had more of Heaven than Hell:
Only there was a handsome picture by,
To which he lent a corner of his eye.
As sin in Greece a prophet was before,
And in old Rome a mighty emperor;

So now being priest he plainly did profess
To make a jest of Christ's three offices:
The rather since his scattered jugglings were
United now in one both time and sphere.
From Egypt he took petty deities,
From Greece oracular infallibilities,
And from Old Rome the liberty of pleasure,
By free dispensings of the Church's treasure.
Then in memorial of his ancient throne,
He did surname his palace, Babylon.
Yet that he might the better gain all nations,
And make that name good by their transmigrations;
From all these places, but at divers times,
He took fine vizards to conceal his crimes:
From Egypt anchorism and retiredness,
Learning from Greece, from old Rome stateliness;
And blending these, he carried all men's eyes,
While Truth sat by, counting his victories:
Whereby he grew apace and scorned to use
Such force as once did captivate the Jews;
But did bewitch, and finally work each nation
Into a voluntary transmigration.
All post to Rome: Princes submit their necks
Either to his public foot or private tricks.
It did not fit his gravity to stir,
Nor his long journey, nor his gout and fur:
Therefore he sent out able ministers,
Statesmen within, without doors cloisterers;
Who without spear, or sword, or other drum,
Than what was in their tongue, did overcome;
And having conquered, did so strangely rule,
That the whole world did seem but the Pope's mule.
As new and old Rome did one empire twist;
So both together are one Antichrist;
Yet with two faces, as their Janus was,
Being in this their old cracked looking-glass.

"How dear to me, O God, Thy counsels are!
              Who may with Thee compare?"
Thus sin triumphs in western Babylon;
Yet not as sin, but as religion.
Of his two thrones he made the latter best,
And to defray his journey from the east
Old and new Babylon are to hell and night,
As is the moon and sun to Heaven and light.
When the one did set, the other did take place,
Confronting equally the law and grace.
They are hell's land-marks, Satan's double crest:
They are sin's nipples, feeding the east and west.
But as in vice the copy still exceeds
The pattern, but not so in virtuous deeds;
So though sin made his latter seat the better,
The latter Church is to the first a debtor.
The second Temple could not reach the first:
And the late reformation never durst
Compare with ancient times and purer years;
But in the Jews and us deserveth tears;
Nay, it shall every year decrease and fade;
Till such a darkness do the world invade
At Christ's last coming, as His first did find:
Yet must there such proportions be assigned
To these diminishings, as is between
The spacious world and Jewry to be seen.
Religion stands on tiptoe in our land,
Ready to pass to the American strand.
When height of malice, and prodigious lusts,
Impudent sinning, witchcrafts, and distrusts,
(The marks of future bane,) shall fill our cup
Unto the brim, and make our measure up;
When Seine shall swallow Tiber, and the Thames
By letting in them both, pollutes her streams:
When Italy of us shall have her will,
And all her calendar of sins fulfil;

o

Whereby one may foretell what sins next year
Shall both in France and England domineer:
Then shall religion to America flee:
They have their times of Gospel, e'en as we.
My God, Thou dost prepare for them a way,
By carrying first their gold from them away:
For gold and grace did never yet agree:
Religion always sides with poverty.
We think we rob them, but we think amiss:
We are more poor, and they more rich by this.
Thou wilt revenge their quarrel, making grace
To pay our debts, and leave our ancient place
To go to them, while that, which now their nation
But lends to us, shall be our desolation.
Yet as the Church shall thither westward fly,
So sin shall trace and dog her instantly:
They have their period also and set times
Both for their virtuous actions and their crimes.
And where of old the empire and the arts
Ushered the Gospel ever in men's hearts,
Spain hath done one; when arts perform the other,
The Church shall come, and sin the Church shall
        smother:
That when they have accomplished the round,
And met in the east their first and ancient sound,
Judgment may meet them both and search them round.
Thus do both lights, as well in Church as sun,
Light one another, and together run.
Thus also sin and darkness follow still
The Church and sun with all their power and skill.
But as the sun still goes both west and east,
So also did the Church by going west
Still eastward go; because it drew more near
To time and place, where judgement shall appear.
" How dear to me, O God, Thy counsels are!
        Who may with Thee compare?"

L'ENVOY

KING of glory, King of peace,
  With the one make war to cease;
With the other bless Thy sheep,
Thee to love, in Thee to sleep.
Let not sin devour Thy fold,
Bragging that Thy blood is cold;
That Thy death is also dead,
While his conquests daily spread;
That Thy flesh hath lost his food,
And Thy cross is common wood.
Choke him, let him say no more,
But reserve his breath in store,
Till Thy conquest and his fall
Make his sighs to use it all;
And then bargain with the wind
To discharge what is behind.

Blessed be God alone,
Thrice blessed Three in One.

Miscellaneous Poems

A SONNET

SENT BY GEORGE HERBERT TO HIS MOTHER AS A NEW YEAR'S GIFT
FROM CAMBRIDGE

M Y God, where is that ancient heat towards Thee,
   Wherewith whole shoals of Martyrs once did
      burn,
Besides their other flames?   Doth poetry
   Wear Venus' livery? only serve her turn?
Why are not sonnets made of Thee? and lays
   Upon Thine altar burnt?   Cannot Thy love
Heighten a spirit to sound out Thy praise
   As well as any she?   Cannot Thy Dove
Outstrip their Cupid easily in flight?
   Or, since Thy ways are deep, and still the same,
   Will not a verse run smooth that bears Thy name?
Why doth that fire, which by Thy power and might
   Each breast does feel, no braver fuel choose
   Than that, which one day, worms may chance refuse.
Sure, Lord, there is enough in Thee to dry
   Oceans of ink; for as the deluge did
Cover the earth, so doth Thy Majesty:
   Each cloud distils Thy praise, and doth forbid
Poets to turn it to another use.
   Roses and lilies speak Thee; and to make
A pair of cheeks of them, is thy abuse.
   Why should I women's eyes for crystal take?

Such poor invention burns in their low mind
  Whose fire is wild, and doth not upward go
  To praise, and on Thee, Lord, some ink bestow.
Open the bones, and you shall nothing find
In the best faith but filth; when, Lord, in Thee
The beauty lies in the discovery.

INSCRIPTION IN THE PARSONAGE, BEMERTON

TO MY SUCCESSOR

IF thou chance for to find
  A new house to thy mind
And built without thy cost:
  Be good to the poor,
  As God gives thee store,
And then my labour's not lost.

ON LORD DANVERS

SACRED marble, safely keep
  His dust, who under thee must sleep,
Until the years again restore
  Their dead, and time shall be no more.
Meanwhile, if he (which all things wears)
Does ruin thee, or if thy tears
Are shed for him; dissolve thy frame,
Thou art requited : for his fame,
His virtue, and his worth shall be
Another monument to thee.

A PARADOX

THAT THE SICK ARE IN A BETTER CASE THAN THE WHOLE

YOU who admire yourselves because
    You neither groan nor weep,
And think it contrary to nature's laws
    To want one ounce of sleep,
      Your strong belief
Acquits yourselves, and gives the sick all grief.

Your state to ours is contrary,
    That makes you think us poor,
So Black-moors think us foul, and we
    Are quit with them, and more,
      Nothing can see,
And judge of things but mediocrity.

The sick are in themselves a state
    Which health hath nought to do.
How know you that our tears proceed from woe,
    And not from better fate ?
      Since that mirth hath
Her waters also and desired bath.

How know you that the sighs we send
    From want of breath proceed,
Not from excess : and therefore we do spend
    That which we do not need ;
      So trembling may
As well show inward warbling, as decay.

Cease then to judge calamities
        By outward form and shew,
But view yourselves, and inward turn your eyes,
        Then you shall fully know
                That your estate
Is, of the two, the far more desperate.

You always fear to feel those smarts
        Which we but sometimes prove,
Each little comfort much affects our hearts,
        None but gross joys you move:
                Why then confess
Your fears in number more, your joys are less.

Then for yourselves not us embrace
        Plaints to bad fortune due,
For though you visit us, and plaint our case,
        We doubt much whether you
                Come to our bed
To comfort us, or to be comforted.

Jacula Prudentum

OR

OUTLANDISH PROVERBS, SENTENCES, Etc.

JACULA PRUDENTUM

MAN proposeth, God disposeth.
   Old men go to death, Death comes to young
   men.
He begins to die, that quits his desires.
A handful of good life is better than a bushel of
   learning.
He that studies his content, wants it.
Every day brings its bread with it.
Humble hearts have humble desires.
He that stumbles and falls not, mends his pace.
The house shows the owner.
He that gets out of debt, grows rich.
All is well with him who is beloved of his neighbours.
Building and marrying of children are great wasters.
A good bargain is a pick-purse.
The scalded dog fears cold water.
Pleasing ware is half sold.
Light burdens, long borne, grow heavy.
The wolf knows what the ill beast thinks.
Who hath none to still him may weep out his eyes.
When all sins grow old, covetousness is young.
If ye would know a knave, give him a staff.
You cannot know wine by the barrel.
A cool mouth, and warm feet, live long.
A horse made, and a man to make.
Look not for musk in a dog's kennel.
Not a long day, but a good heart, rids work.

He pulls with a long rope that waits for another's
  death.
Great strokes make not sweet music.
A cask and an ill custom must be broken.
A fat housekeeper makes lean executors.
Empty chambers make foolish maids.
The gentle hawk half maws herself.
The Devil is not always at one door.
When a friend asks, there is no to-morrow.
God sends cold according to clothes.
One sound blow will serve to undo us all.
He loseth nothing, that loseth not God.
The German's wit is in his fingers.
At dinner my man appears.
Who gives to all, denies all.
Quick believers need broad shoulders.
Who remove stones, bruise their fingers.
Benefits please like flowers while they are fresh.
Between the business of life and the day of death a
    space ought to be interposed.
All came from, and will go to others.
He that will take a bird, must not scare it.
He lives unsafely that looks too near on things.
A gentle housewife mars the household,
A crooked log makes a straight fire.
He hath great need of a fool that plays the fool him-
A merchant that gains not, loseth.   [self.
Let not him that fears feathers come among wild-fowl.
Love, and a cough, cannot be hid.
A dwarf on a giant's shoulder sees further of the two.
He that sends a fool means to follow him.
Brabbling curs never want sore ears.
Better the feet slip than the tongue.
For washing his hands, none sells his lands.
A lion's skin is never cheap.
The goat must browse where she is tied.

Nothing is to be presumed on, or despaired of.
Who hath a wolf for his mate needs a dog for his man.
In a good house all is quickly ready.
A bad dog never sees the wolf.
God oft hath a great share in a little house.
Ill ware is never cheap.
A cheerful look makes a dish a feast,
If all fools had baubles, we should want fuel.
Virtue never grows old.
Evening words are not like to morning.
Were there no fools, bad ware would not pass.
Never had ill workman good tools.
He stands not surely that never slips.
Were there no hearers, there would be no back-biters.
Everything is of use to a housekeeper.
When prayers are done, my lady is ready.
Cities seldom change religion only.
At length the fox turns monk.
Flies are busiest about lean horses.
Hearken to reason, or she will be heard.
The bird loves her nest.
Everything new is fine.
When a dog is a drowning, every one offers him drink.
Better a bare foot than none.
Who is so deaf as he that will not hear?
He that is warm thinks all so.
At length the fox is brought to the furrier.
He that goes barefoot must not plant thorns.
They that are booted are not always ready.
He that will learn to pray, let him go to sea.
In spending lies the advantage.
He that lives well, is learned enough.
Ill vessels seldom miscarry.
A full belly neither fights nor flies well.
All truths are not to be told.

An old wise man's shadow is better than a young
    buzzard's sword.
Noble housekeepers need no doors.
Every ill man hath his ill day.
Sleep without supping, and wake without owing.
I gave the mouse a hole, and she is become my heir.
Assail who will, the valiant attends.
Whither goest, Grief?   Where I am wont.
Praise day at night, and life at the end.
Whither shall the ox go where he shall not labour?
Where you think there is bacon, there is no chimney.
Mend your clothes, and you may hold out this year.
Press a stick, and it seems a youth.
The tongue walks where the teeth speed not.
A fair wife and a frontier castle breed quarrels.
Leave jesting whiles it pleaseth, lest it turn to earnest.
Deceive not thy physician, confessor, nor lawyer.
Ill natures, the more you ask them, the more they stick.
Virtue and a trade are the best portion for children.
The chicken is the country's, but the city eats it.
He that gives thee a capon, give him the leg and the
    wing.
He that lives ill, fear follows him.
Give a clown your finger, and he will take your hand.
Good is to be sought out, and evil attended.
A good paymaster starts not at assurances.
No alchymy to saving.
To a grateful man give money when he asks.
Who would do ill ne'er wants occasion.
To fine folks a little ill finely wrapt.
A child correct behind, and not before.
To a fair day, open the window, but make you ready
    as to a foul one.
Keep good men company, and you shall be of the
    number.
No love to a father's.

The mill gets by going.
To a boiling pot flies come not.
Make haste to an ill way, that you may get out of it.
A snow year a rich year.
Better to be blind than to see ill.
Learn weeping, and thou shalt laugh gaining.
Who hath no more bread than need must not keep
a dog.
A garden must be looked unto and dressed as the body.
The fox when he cannot reach the grapes, says they
are not ripe.
Water trotted is as good as oats.
Though the mastiff be gentle, yet bite him not by the
lip.
Though a lie be well dressed, it is ever overcome.
Though old and wise, yet still advise.
Three helping one another bear the burden of six.
Slander is a shipwreck by a dry tempest.
Old wine and an old friend are good provisions.
Happy is he that chastens himself.
Well may he smell fire whose gown burns.
The wrongs of a husband or master are not reproached.
Welcome evil, if thou comest alone.
Love your neighbour, yet pull not down your hedge.
The bit that one eats no friend makes.
A drunkard's purse is a bottle.
She spins well that breeds her children.
Good is the *mora*[1] that makes all sure.
Play with a fool at home, and he will play with you
in the market.
Every one stretcheth his legs according to his cover-
let.
Autumnal agues are long or mortal.
Marry your son when you will; your daughter when
you can.

[1] Delay.

Dally not with money or women.
Men speak of the fair as things went with them there.
The best remedy against an ill man is much ground
    between both.
The mill cannot grind with the water that's past.
Corn is cleaned with wind, and the soul with chasten-
    ings.
Good words are worth much, and cost little.
To buy dear is not bounty.
Jest not with the eye, or with religion.
The eye and religion can bear no jesting.
Without favour none will know you, and with it you
    will not know yourself.
Buy at a fair, but sell at home.
Cover yourself with your shield, and care not for cries.
A wicked man's gift hath a touch of his master.
None is a fool always, every one sometimes.
From a choleric man withdraw a little, from him
    that says nothing for ever.
Debtors are liars.
Of all smells, bread: of all tastes, salt.
In a great river great fish are found: but take heed
    lest you be drowned.
Ever since we wear clothes, we know not one another.
God heals, and the physician hath the thanks.
Hell is full of good meanings and wishings.
Take heed of still waters, the quick pass away.
After the house is finished, leave it.
Our own actions are our security, not others' judg-
    ments.
Think of ease, but work on.
He that lies long a bed, his estate feels it.
Whether you boil snow or pound it, you can have
    but water of it.
One stroke fells not an oak.
God complains not, but doth what is fitting.

A diligent scholar, and the master's paid.
Milk says to wine, Welcome, friend.
They that know one another salute afar off.
Where there is no honour there is no grief.
Where the drink goes in there the wit goes out.
He that stays does the business.
Alms never make poor.   [Or thus,]
Great almsgiving lessens no man's living.
Giving much to the poor doth enrich a man's store.
It takes much from the account, to which his sin
    doth amount.
It adds to the glory both of soul and body.
Ill comes in by ells, and goes out by inches.
The smith and his penny both are black.
Whose house is of glass must not throw stones at
    another.
If the old dog bark, he gives counsel.
The tree that grows slowly keeps itself for another.
I wept when I was born, and every day shews why.
He that looks not before finds himself behind.
He that plays his money ought not to value it.
He that riseth first is first drest.
Diseases of the eye are to be cured with the elbow.
The hole calls the thief.
A gentleman's greyhound and a saltbox, seek them
    at the fire.
A child's service is little, yet he is no little fool that
    despiseth it.
The river past, and God forgotten.
Evils have their comfort: good none can support
    (to wit) with a moderate and contented heart.
Who must account for himself and others must
    know both.
He that eats the hard shall eat the ripe.   .
The miserable man maketh a penny of a farthing,
    and the liberal of a farthing sixpence.

The honey is sweet, but the bee stings.
Weight and measure take away strife.
The son full and tattered, the daughter empty and
　　fine.
Every path hath a puddle.
In good years corn is hay, in ill years straw is corn.
Send a wise man on an errand, and say nothing
　　unto him.
In life you loved me not, in death you bewail me.
Into a mouth shut flies fly not.
The heart's letter is read in the eyes.
The ill that comes out of our mouth falls into our
　　bosom.
In great pedigrees there are governors and chandlers.
In the house of a fiddler all fiddle.
Sometimes the best gain is to lose.
Working and making a fire doth discretion require.
One grain fills not a sack, but helps his fellows.
It is a great victory that comes without blood.
In war, hunting, and love, men for one pleasure a
　　thousand griefs prove.
Reckon right, and February hath one and thirty days.
Honour without profit is a ring on the finger.
Estate in two parishes is bread in two wallets.
Honour and profit lie not in one sack.
A naughty child is better sick than whole.
Truth and oil are ever above.
He that riseth betimes hath something in his head.
Advise none to marry or go to war.
To steal the hog, and give the feet for alms.
The thorn comes forth with his point forwards.
One hand washeth another, and both the face.
The fault of the horse is put on the saddle.
The corn hides itself in the snow as an old man in furs.
The Jews spend at Easter, the Moors at marriages,
　　the Christians in suits.

Fine dressing is a foul house swept before the doors.

A woman and a glass are ever in danger.

An ill wound is cured, not an ill name.

The wise hand doth not all that the foolish mouth speaks.

On painting and fighting look aloof.

Knowledge is folly, except grace guide it.

Punishment is lame, but it comes.

The more women look in their glass, the less they look to their house.

A long tongue is a sign of a short hand.

Marry a widow before she leave mourning.

The worst of law is, that one suit breeds twenty.

Providence is better than a rent.

What your glass tells you will not be told by counsel.

There are more men threatened than stricken.

A fool knows more in his house than a wise man in another's.

I had rather ride on an ass that carries me than a horse that throws me.

The hard gives more than he that hath nothing.

The beast that goes always never wants blows.

Good cheap is dear.

It costs more to do ill than to do well.

Good words quench more than a bucket of water.

An ill agreement is better than a good judgment.

There is more talk than trouble.

Better spare to have of thine own than ask of other men.

Better good afar off than evil at hand.

Fear keeps the garden better than the gardener.

I had rather ask of my sire brown bread than borrow of my neighbour white.

Your pot broken seems better than my whole one.

Let an ill man lie in thy straw and he looks to be thy heir.

By suppers more have been killed than Galen ever
   cured.
While the discreet advise, the fool doth his business.
A mountain and a river are good neighbours.
Gossips are frogs, they drink and talk.
Much spends the traveller more than the abider.
Prayers and provender hinder no journey.
A well bred youth neither speaks of himself, nor
   being spoken to, is silent.
A journeying women speaks much of all, and all of
   her.
The fox knows much, but more he that catcheth him.
Many friends in general, one in special.
The fool asks much, but he is more fool that grants
   it.
Many kiss the hand they wish cut off.
Neither bribe, nor lose thy right.
In the world who knows not to swim goes to the
   bottom.
Choose not a house near an inn (viz. for noise), or
   in a corner (for filth).
He is a fool that thinks not that another thinks.
Neither eyes on letters, nor hands in coffers.
The lion is not so fierce as they paint him.
Go not for every grief to the physician, nor for every
   quarrel to the lawyer, nor for every thirst to the
   pot.
Good service is a great enchantment.
There would be no great ones if there were no little
   ones.
It is no sure rule to fish with a cross-bow.
There were no ill language if it were not ill taken.
The groundsel speaks not, save what it heard at the
   hinges.
The best mirror is an old friend.
Say no ill of the year till it be past.

A man's discontent is his worst evil.

Fear nothing but sin.

The child says nothing but what it heard by the fire.

Call me not an olive till thou see me gathered.

That is not good language which all understand not.

He that burns his house warms himself for once.

He will burn his house to warm his hands.

He will spend a whole year's rent at one meal's meat.

All is not gold that glisters.

A blustering night, a fair day.

Be not idle, and you shall not be longing.

He is not poor that hath little, but he that desireth much.

Let none say, I will not drink water.

He wrongs not an old man that steals his supper from him.

The tongue talks at the head's cost.

He that strikes with his tongue must ward with his head.

Keep not ill men company, lest you increase the number.

God strikes not with both hands, for to the sea He made heavens, and to rivers fords.

A rugged stone grows smooth from hand to hand.

No lock will hold against the power of gold.

The absent party is still faulty.

Peace and patience, and death with repentance.

If you lose your time, you cannot get money nor gain.

Be not a baker if your head be of butter.

Ask much to have a little.

Little sticks kindle the fire; great ones put it out.

Another's bread costs dear.

Although it rain, throw not away thy watering-pot.

Although the sun shine, leave not thy cloak at home.

A little with quiet is the only diet.

In vain is the mill-clack, if the miller his hearing lack.

By the needle you shall draw the thread, and by that which is past see how that which is to come will be drawn on.

Stay a little, and news will find you.

Stay till the lame messenger come, if you will know the truth of the thing.

When God will, no wind but brings rain.

Though you rise early, yet the day comes at his time and not till then.

Pull down your hat on the wind's side.

As the year is, your pot must seethe.

Since you know all, and I nothing, tell me what I dreamed last night.

When the fox preacheth, beware geese.

When you are an anvil, hold you still; when you are a hammer, strike your fill.

Poor and liberal, rich and covetous.

He that makes his bed ill, lies there.

He that labours and thrives, spins gold.

He that sows, trusts in God.

He that lies with the dogs, riseth with fleas.

He that repairs not a part, builds all.

A discontented man knows not where to sit easy.

Who spits against heaven, it falls in his face.

He that dines and leaves, lays the cloth twice.

Who eats his cock alone, must saddle his horse alone.

He that is not handsome at twenty, nor strong at thirty, nor rich at forty, nor wise at fifty, will never be handsome, strong, rich, or wise.

He that doth what he will, doth not what he ought.

He that will deceive the fox must rise betimes.

He that lives well sees afar off.

He that hath a mouth of his own, must not say to another, Blow.

He that will be served must be patient.

He that gives thee a bone would not have thee die.
He that chastens one chastens twenty.
He that hath lost his credit is dead to the world.
He that hath no ill fortune is troubled with good.
He that demands misseth not, unless his demands
    be foolish.
He that hath no honey in his pot let him have it in
    his mouth.
He that takes not up a pin slights his wife.
He that owes nothing, if he makes not mouths at us,
    is courteous.
He that loseth his due gets not thanks.
He that believes all misseth; he that believeth
    nothing hits not.
Pardons and pleasantness are great revenges of
    slander.
A married man turns his staff into a stake.
If you would know secrets look them in grief or
    pleasure.
Serve a noble disposition, though poor, the time
    comes that he will repay thee.
The fault is as great as he that is faulty.
If folly were grief, every house would weep.
He that would be well old must be old betimes.
Sit in your place, and none can make you rise.
If you could run as you drink you might catch a
    hare.
Would you know what money is, go borrow some.
The morning sun never lasts a day.
Thou hast death in thy house and dost bewail
    another's.
All griefs with bread are less.
All things require skill but an appetite.
All things have their place knew we how to place
    them.
Little pitchers have wide ears.

We are fools one to another.
This world is nothing except it tend to another.
There are three ways, the universities, the sea, the
  court.
God comes to see without a bell.
Life without a friend is death without a witness.
Clothe thee in war, arm thee in peace.
The horse thinks one thing, and he that saddles him
  another.
Mills and wives ever want.
The dog that licks ashes trust not with meal.
The buyer needs a hundred eyes, the seller not
  one.
He carries well, to whom it weighs not.
The comforter's head never aches.
Step after step the ladder is ascended.
Who likes not the drink, God deprives him of bread.
To a crazy ship all winds are contrary.
Justice pleaseth few in their own house.
In time comes he whom God sends.
Water afar off quencheth not fire.
In sports and journeys men are known.
An old friend is a new house.
Love is not found in the market.
Dry feet, warm head, bring safe to bed.
He is rich enough that wants nothing.
One father is enough to govern one hundred sons,
  but not a hundred sons one father.
Far shooting never killed bird.
An upbraided morsel never choked any.
Dearths foreseen come not.
An ill labourer quarrels with his tools.
He that falls into the dirt, the longer he stays there
  the fouler he is.
He that blames would buy.
He that sings on Friday will weep on Sunday.

The charges of building and making of gardens are
  unknown.
My house, my house, though thou art small, thou
  art to me the Escurial.
A hundred load of thought will not pay one of debts.
He that comes of a hen must scrape.
He that seeks trouble never misses.
He that once deceives is ever suspected.
Being on sea, sail; being on land, settle.
Who doth his own business fouls not his hands.
He that makes a good war makes a good peace.
He that works after his own manner his head aches
  not at the matter.
Who hath bitter in his mouth spits not all sweet.
He that hath children all his morsels are not his
  own.
He that hath the spice may season as he list.
He that hath a head of wax must not walk in the
  sun.
He that hath love in his breast hath spurs in his
  side.
He that respects not is not respected.
He that hath a fox for his mate hath need of a net at
  his girdle.
He that hath right fears; he that hath wrong hopes.
He that hath patience hath fat thrushes for a farth-
  ing.
Never was strumpet fair.
He that measures not himself is measured.
He that hath one hog makes him fat; and he that
  hath one son makes him a fool.
Who lets his wife go to every feast, and his horse
  drink at every water, shall neither have good
  wife nor good horse.
He that speaks sows, and he that holds his peace
  gathers.

He that hath little is the lest dirty.
He that lives most dies most.
He that hath one foot in the straw hath another in the spital.
He that is fed at another's hand may stay long ere he be full.
He that makes a thing too fine breaks it.
He that bewails himself hath the cure in his hands.
He that would be well needs not go from his own house.
Counsel breaks not the head.
Fly the pleasure that bites to-morrow.
He that knows what may be gained in a day never steals.
Money refused loseth its brightness.
Health and money go far.
Where your will is ready your feet are light.
A great ship asks deep waters.
Woe to the house where there is no chiding.
Take heed of the vinegar of sweet wine.
Fools bite one another, but wise men agree together.
Trust not one night's ice.
Good is good, but better carries it.
To gain teacheth how to spend.
Good finds good.
The dog gnaws the bone because he cannot swallow it.
The crow bewails the sheep, and then eats it.
Building is a sweet impoverishing.
The first degree of folly is to hold one's self wise, the second to profess it, the third to despise counsel.
The greatest step is that out of doors.
To weep for joy is a kind of manna.
The first service a child doeth his father is to make him foolish.
The resolved mind hath no cares.

In the kingdom of a cheater the wallet is carried
before.
The eye will have his part.
The good mother says not, Will you? but gives.
A house and a woman suit excellently.
In the kingdom of blind men the one-eyed is king.
A little kitchen makes a large house.
War makes thieves, and peace hangs them.
Poverty is the mother of health.
In the morning mountains, in the evening fountains.
The back door robs the house.
Wealth is like rheum, it falls on the weakest parts.
The gown is his that wears it, and the world his
that enjoys it.
Hope is the poor man's bread.
Virtue now is in herbs, and stones, and words only.
Fine words dress ill deeds.
Labour is long lived, pray as even dying.
A poor beauty finds more lovers than husbands.
Discreet women have neither eyes nor ears.
Things well fitted abide.
Prettiness dies first.
Talking pays no toll.
The master's eye fattens the horse, and his foot the
ground,
Disgraces are like cherries, one draws another.
Praise a hill, but keep below.
Praise the sea, but keep on land.
In choosing a wife, and buying a sword, we ought
not to trust another.
The wearer knows where the shoe wrings.
Fair is not fair, but that which pleaseth.
There is no jollity but hath a smack of folly.
He that's long a giving knows not how to give.
The filth under the white snow the sun discovers.
Every one fastens where there is gain.

All feet tread not in one shoe.

Patience, time, and money accommodate all things.

For want of a nail the shoe is lost, for want of a shoe the horse is lost, for want of a horse the rider is lost.

Weigh justly, and sell dearly.

Little wealth little care.

Little journeys and good cost bring safe home.

Gluttony kills more than the sword.

When children stand quiet they have done some ill.

A little and good fills the trencher.

A penny spared is twice got.

When a knave is in a plum-tree he hath neither friend nor kin.

Short boughs long vintage.

Health without money is half an ague.

If the wise erred not it would go hard with fools.

Bear with evil and expect good. `

He that tells a secret is another's servant.

If all fools wore white caps we should seem a flock of geese.

Water, fire and soldiers quickly make room.

Pension never enriched a young man.

Under water, famine; under snow, bread.

The lame goes as far as your staggerer.

He that loseth is merchant as well as he that gains.

A jade eats as much as a good horse.

All things in their being are good for something.

One flower makes no garland.

A fair death honours the whole life.

One enemy is too much.

Living well is the best revenge.

One fool makes a hundred.

One pair of ears draws dry a hundred tongues.

A fool may throw a stone into a well, which a hundred wise men cannot pull out.

One slumber finds another.
On a good bargain think twice.
To a good spender God is the treasurer.
A curst cow hath short horns.
Music helps not the toothache.
We cannot come to honour under coverlet.
Great pains quickly find ease.
To the counsel of fools a wooden bell.
The choleric man never wants woe.
Help thyself, and God will help thee.
At the game's end we shall see who gains.
There are many ways to fame.
Love is the true price of love.
Love rules his kingdom without a sword.
Love makes all hard hearts gentle.
Love makes a good eye squint.
Love asks faith, and faith firmness.
A sceptre is one thing, and a ladle another.
Great trees are good for nothing but shade.
He commands enough that obeys a wise man.
Fair words make me look to my purse.
Though the fox run the chicken hath wings.
He plays well that wins.
You must strike in measure, when there are many
    to strike on one anvil.
The shortest answer is doing.
It is a poor stake that cannot stand one year in the
    ground.
He that commits a fault thinks every one speaks of
    it.
He that is foolish in the fault let him be wise in the
    punishment.
The blind eats many a fly.
He that can make a fire well can end a quarrel.
The toothache is more ease than to deal with ill
    people.

He that would have what he hath not should do what he doth not.

He that hath no good trade it is to his loss.

The offender never pardons.

He that lives not well one year sorrows seven after.

He that hopes not for good fears not evil.

He that is angry at a feast is rude.

He that mocks a cripple ought to be whole.

When the tree is fallen all go with their hatchet.

He that hath horns in his bosom let him not put them on his head.

He that burns most shines most.

He that trusts in a lie shall perish in truth.

He that blows in the dust fills his eyes with it.

Bells call others, but themselves enter not into the church.

Of fair things the autumn is fair.

Giving is dead, restoring very sick.

A gift much expected is paid, not given.

Two ill meals make the third a glutton.

The Royal Crown cures not the headache.

'Tis hard to be wretched, but worse to be known so.

A feather in hand is better than a bird in the air.

It is better to be the head of a lizard than the tail of a lion.

Good and quickly seldom meet.

Folly grows without watering.

Happier are the hands compassed with iron, than a heart with thoughts.

If the staff be crooked, the shadow cannot be straight.

To take the nuts from the fire with the dog's foot.

He is a fool that makes a wedge of his fist.

Valour that parleys is near yielding.

Thursday come, and the week is gone.

A flatterer's throat is an open sepulchre.

There is great force hidden in a sweet command.
The command of custom is great.
To have money is a fear, not to have it a grief.
The cat sees not the mouse ever.
Little dogs start the hare, the great get her.
Willows are weak, yet they bind other wood.
A good payer is master of another's purse.
The thread breaks where it is weakest.
Old men, when they scorn young make much of death.
God is at the end, when we think he is furthest off it.
A good judge conceives quickly, judges slowly.
Rivers need a spring.
He that contemplates hath a day without night.
Give losers leave to talk.
Loss embraceth shame.
Gaming, women, and wine, while they laugh, they make men pine.
The fat man knoweth not what the lean thinketh.
Wood half burnt is easily kindled.
The fish adores the bait.
He that goeth far hath many encounters.
Every bee's honey is sweet.
The slothful is the servant of the counters.
Wisdom hath one foot on land and another on the sea.
The thought hath good legs, and the quill a good tongue.
A wise man needs not blush for changing his purpose.
The March sun raises, but dissolves not.
Time is the rider that breaks youth.
The wine in the bottle doth not quench thirst.
The sight of a man hath the force of a lion.
An examined enterprise goes on boldly.
In every art it is good to have a master.
In every country dogs bite.

Q

In every country the sun rises in the morning.
A noble plant suits not with a stubborn ground.
You may bring a horse to the river, but he will
    drink when and what he pleaseth.
Before you make a friend, eat a bushel of salt with
    him.
Speak fitly, or be silent wisely.
Skill and confidence are an unconquered army.
I was taken by a morsel, says the fish.
A disarmed peace is weak.
The balance distinguisheth not between gold and
    lead.
The persuasion of the fortunate sways the doubtful.
To be beloved is above all bargains.
To deceive oneself is very easy.
The reasons of the poor weigh not.
Perverseness makes one squint-eyed.
The evening praises the day, and the morning a frost.
The table robs more than a thief.
When age is jocund it makes sport for death.
True praise roots and spreads.
Fears are divided in the midst.
The soul needs few things, the body many.
Astrology is true but the astrologers cannot find it.
Tie it well, and let it go.
Empty vessels sound most.
Send not a cat for lard.
Foolish tongues talk by the dozen.
Love makes one fit for any work.
A pitiful mother makes a scald head.
An old physician, and a young lawyer.
Talk much and err much, says the Spaniard.
Some make a conscience of spitting in the Church,
    yet rob the altar.
An idle head is a box for the wind.
Show me a liar, and I will show thee a thief.

A bean in liberty is better than a comfit in prison.

None is born master.

Show a good man his error, and he turns it to a
   virtue; but an ill, it doubles his fault.

None is offended but by himself.

None says his garner is full.

In the husband wisdom, in the wife gentleness.

Nothing dries sooner than a tear.

In a leopard the spots are not observed.

Nothing lasts but the Church.

A wise man cares not for what he cannot have.

It is not good fishing before the net.

He cannot be virtuous that is not rigorous.

That which will not be spun, let it not come between
   the spindle and the distaff.

When my house burns, it is not good playing at chess.

No barber shaves so close but another finds work.

There is no great banquet, but some fares ill.

A holy habit cleanseth not a foul soul.

Forbear not sowing because of birds.

Mention not a halter in the house of him that was
   hanged.

Speak not of a dead man at the table.

A hat is not made for one shower.

No sooner is a temple built to God but the devil
   builds a chapel hard by.

Every one puts his fault on the times.

You cannot make a windmill go with a pair of bellows.

Pardon all but thyself.

Every one is weary, the poor in seeking, the rich in
   keeping, the good in learning.

The escaped mouse ever feels the taste of the bait.

A little wind kindles, much puts out the fire.

Dry bread at home is better than roast meat abroad.

More have repented speech than silence.

The covetous spends more than the liberal.

Divine ashes are better than earthly meal.
Beauty draws more than oxen.
One father is more than a hundred schoolmasters.
One eye of the master's sees more than ten of the
    servant's.
When God will punish He will first take away the
    understanding.
A little labour much health.
When it thunders the thief becomes honest.
The tree that God plants no wind hurts it.
Knowledge is no burden.
It is a bold mouse that nestles in the cat's ear.
Long jesting was never good.
If a good man thrive, all thrive with him.
If the mother had not been in the oven she had
    never sought her daughter there.
If great men would have care of little ones both
    would last long.
Though you see a churchman ill, yet continue in
    the church still.
Old praise dies, unless you feed it.
If things were to be done twice, all would be wise.
Had you the world on your chess-board, you could
    not fill all to your mind.
Suffer and expect.
If fools should not fool it, they should lose their
    season.
Love and business teach eloquence.
That which two will takes effect.
He complains wrongfully of the sea, that twice
    suffers shipwreck.
He is only bright that shines by himself.
A valiant man's look is more than a coward's sword.
The effect speaks, the tongue needs not.
Divine grace was never slow.
Reason lies between the spur and the bridle.

It is a proud horse that will not carry his own pro-
vender.
Three women make a market.
Three can hold their peace if two be away.
It is an ill counsel that hath no escape.
All our pomp the earth covers.
To whirl the eyes too much shows a kite's brain.
Comparisons are odious.
All keys hang not on one girdle.
Great businesses turn on a little pin.
The wind in one's face makes one wise.
All the arms of England will not arm fear.
One sword keeps another in the sheath.
Be what thou would'st seem to be.
Let all live as they would die.
A gentle heart is tied with an easy thread.
Sweet discourse makes short days and nights.
God provides for him that trusteth.
He that will not have peace God gives him war.
To him that will, ways are not wanting.
To a great night a great lanthorn.
To a child all weather is cold.
Where there is peace God is.
None is so wise but the fool overtakes him.
Fools give to please all but their own.
Prosperity lets go the bridle.
The friar preached against stealing, and had a goose
in his sleeve.
To be too busy gets contempt.
February makes a bridge, and March breaks it.
A horse stumbles that hath four legs.
The best smell is bread, the best savour salt, the
best love that of children.
That's the best gown that goes up and down the
house.
The market is the best garden.

The first dish pleaseth all.
The higher the ape goes the more he shows his tail.
Night is the mother of councils.
God's mill grinds slow, but sure.
Every one thinks his sack heaviest.
Drought never brought dearth.
All complain.
Gamesters and race-horses never last long.
It is a poor sport that is not worth the candle.
He that is fallen cannot help him that is down.
Every one is witty for his own purpose.
A little let lets an ill workman.
Good workmen are seldom rich.
By doing nothing we learn to do ill.
A great dowry is a bed full of brambles.
No profit to honour, no honour to religion.
Every sin brings its punishment with it.
Of him that speaks ill, consider the life more than
    the word.
You cannot hide an eel in a sack.
Give not Saint *Peter* so much, to leave Saint *Paul*
    nothing.
You cannot flay a stone.
The chief disease that reigns this year is folly.
A sleepy master makes his servant a lout.
Better speak truth rudely, than lie covertly.
He that fears leaves, let him not go into the wood.
One foot is better than two crutches.
Better suffer ill than do ill.
Neither praise nor dispraise thyself, thy actions
    serve the turn.
Soft and fair goes far.
The constancy of the benefit of the year in their
    seasons argues a deity.
Praise none too much, for all are fickle.
It is absurd to warm one in his armour.

Lawsuits consume time, and money, and rest, and friends.

Nature draws more than ten teams.

He that hath a wife and children wants not business.

A ship and a woman are ever repairing.

He that fears death lives not.

He that pities another remembers himself.

He that doth what he should not, shall feel what he would not.

He that marries for wealth sells his liberty.

He that once hits is ever bending.

He that serves must serve.

He that lends gives.

He that preacheth giveth alms.

He that cockers his child provides for his enemy.

A pitiful look asks enough.

Who will sell the cow must say the word.

Service is no inheritance.

The faulty stands on his guard.

A kinsman, a friend, or whom you entreat, take not to serve you if you will be served neatly.

At Court every one for himself.

To a crafty man a crafty and a half.

He that is thrown would ever wrestle.

He that serves well need not ask his wages.

Fair language grates not the tongue.

A good heart cannot lie.

Good swimmers at length are drowned.

Good land, evil way.

In doing we learn.

It is good walking with a horse in one's hand.

God, and parents, and our master, can never be requited.

An ill deed cannot bring honour.

A small heart hath small desires.

All are not merry that dance lightly.

Courtesy on one side only lasts not long.

Wine-counsels seldom prosper.

Weening is not measure.

The best of the sport is to do the deed, and say
nothing.

If thou thyself canst do it, attend no other's help or
hand.

Of a little thing, a little displeaseth.

He warms too near that burns.

God keep me from four houses, a usurer's, a tavern,
a spital, and a prison.

In a hundred ells of contention, there is not an inch
of love.

Do what thou oughtest, and come what come can.

Hunger makes dinners, pastime suppers.

In a long journey straw weighs.

Women laugh when they can, and weep when they
will.

War is death's feast.

Set good against evil.

He that brings good news knocks hard.

Beat the dog before the lion.

Haste comes not alone.

You must lose a fly to catch a trout.

No prison is fair, nor love foul.

He is not free that draws his chain.

He goes not out of his way that goes to a good inn.

There comes nought out of the sack but what was
there.

A little given seasonably excuses a great gift.

He looks not well to himself that looks not ever.

He thinks not well that thinks not again.

Religion, credit, and the eye are not to be touched.

The tongue is not steel, yet it cuts.

A white wall is the paper of a fool.

They talk of Christmas so long that it comes.

That is gold which is worth gold.
It is good tying the sack before it be full.
Words are women, deeds are men.
Poverty is no sin.
A stone in a well is not lost.
He can give little to his servant that licks his knife.
Promising is the eve of giving.
He that keeps his own makes war.
The wolf must die in his own skin.
Goods are theirs that enjoy them.
He that sends a fool expects one.
He that can stay obtains.
He that gains well and spends well needs no account
    book.
He that endures is not overcome.
He that gives all before he dies provides to suffer.
He that talks much of his happiness summons grief.
He that loves the tree loves the branch.
Who hastens a glutton chokes him.
Who praiseth Saint *Peter*, doth not blame Saint
    Paul.
He that hath not the craft let him shut up shop.
He that knows nothing doubts nothing.
Green wood makes a hot fire.
He that marries late marries ill.
He that passeth a winter's day escapes an enemy.
The rich knows not who is his friend.
A morning sun, and a wine-bred child, and a Latin-
    bred woman, seldom end well.
To a close shorn sheep God gives wind by measure.
A pleasure long expected is dear enough sold.
A poor man's cow dies, a rich man's child.
The cow knows not what her tail is worth till she
    have lost it.
Choose a horse made, and a wife to make.
It is an ill air where we gain nothing.

He hath not lived that lives not after death.
So many men in court, and so many strangers.
He quits his place well that leaves his friend there.
That which sufficeth is not little.
Good news may be told at any time, but ill in the
    morning.
He that would be a gentleman let him go to an
    assault.
Who pays the physician does the cure.
None knows the weight of another's burden.
Every one hath a fool in his sleeve.
One hour's sleep before midnight is worth three
    after.
In a retreat the lame are foremost.
It is more pain to do nothing than something.
Amongst good men two men suffice.
There needs a long time to know the world's pulse.
The offspring of those that are very young or very
    old last not.
A tyrant is most tyrant to himself.
Too much taking heed is loss.
Craft against craft makes no living.
The reverend are ever before.
France is a meadow that cuts thrice a year.
It is easier to build two chimneys than to maintain
    one.
The Court hath no almanack.
He that will enter into Paradise must have a good
    key.
When you enter into a house leave the anger ever
    at the door.
He hath no leisure who useth it not.
It is a wicked thing to make a dearth one's garner.
He that deals in the world needs four sieves.
Take heed of an ox before, of a horse behind, of a
    monk on all sides.

The year doth nothing else but open and shut.

The ignorant hath an eagle's wings and an owl's eyes.

There are more physicians in health than drunkards.

The wife is the key of the house.

The law is not the same at morning and at night.

War and physic are governed by the eye.

Half the world knows not how the other half lies.

Death keeps no calendar.

Ships fear fire more than water.

The least foolish is wise.

The chief box of health is time.

Silks and satins put out the fire in the chimney.

The first blow is as much as two.

The life of man is a winter way.

The way is an ill neighbour.

An old man's staff is the rapper of death's door.

Life is half spent before we know what it is.

The singing man keeps his shop in his throat.

The body is more dressed than the soul.

The body is sooner dressed than the soul.

The physician owes all to the patient, but the patient owes nothing to him but a little money.

The little cannot be great unless he devour many.

Time undermines us.

The choleric drinks, the melancholic eats, the phlegmatic sleeps.

The apothecary's mortar spoils the luter's music.

Conversation makes one what he is.

The deaf gains the injury.

Years know more than books.

Wine is a turncoat, first a friend, then an enemy.

Wine ever pays for his lodging.

Wine makes all sorts of creatures at table.

Wine that cost nothing is digested before it be drunk.

Trees eat but once.

Armour is light at table.

Good horses make short miles.

Castles are forests of stones.

The dainties of the great are the tears of the poor.

Parsons are souls' waggoners.

Children when they are little make parents fools,
    when they are great they make them mad.

The master absent, and the house dead.

Dogs are fine in the field.

Sins are not known till they be acted.

Thorns whiten, yet do nothing.

All are presumed good till they are found in a fault.

The great put the little on the hook.

The great would have none great, and the little all
    little.

The Italians are wise before the deed, the Germans
    in the deed, the French after the deed.

Every mile is two in winter.

Spectacles are death's arquebuse.

Lawyers' houses are built on the heads of fools.

The house is a fine house when good folks are within.

The best bred have the best portion.

The first and last frosts are the worst.

Gifts enter everywhere without a wimble.

Princes have no way.

Knowledge makes one laugh, but wealth makes one
    dance.

The citizen is at his business before he rise.

The eyes have one language everywhere.

It is better to have wings than horns.

Better be a fool than a knave.

Count not four, except you have them in a wallet.

To live peaceably with all breeds good blood.

You may be on land, yet not in a garden.

You cannot make the fire so low but it will get out.

We know not who lives or dies.

An ox is taken by the horns, and a man by the
tongue.

Many things are lost for want of asking.

No church-yard is so handsome, that a man would
desire straight to be buried there.

Cities are taken by the ears.

Once a year a man may say, On his conscience.

We leave more to do when we die than we have done.

With customs we live well, but laws undo us.

To speak of a usurer at the table mars the wine.

Pains to get, care to keep, fear to lose.

For a morning rain leave not your journey.

One fair day in winter makes not birds merry.

He that learns a trade hath a purchase made.

When all men have what belongs to them it cannot
be much.

Though God take the sun out of the heaven yet we
must have patience.

When a man sleeps his head is in his stomach.

When one is on horseback he knows all things.

When God is made master of a family He orders
the disorderly.

When a lackey comes to hell's door the devils lock
the gates.

He that is at ease seeks dainties.

He that hath charge of souls transports them not in
bundles.

He that tells his wife news is but newly married.

He that is in a town in May loseth his spring.

He that is in a tavern, thinks he is in a vine-garden.

He that praiseth himself spattereth himself.

He that is a master must serve.

He that is surprised with the first frost feels it all
the winter after.

He a beast doth die that hath done no good to his
country.

He that follows the Lord hopes to go before.

He that dies without the company of good men puts not himself into a good way.

Who hath no head needs no heart.

Who hath no haste in his business mountains to him seem valleys.

Speak not of my debts unless you mean to pay them.

He that is not in the wars is not out of danger.

He that gives me small gifts, would have me live.

He that is his own counsellor knows nothing sure but what he hath laid out.

He that hath lands hath quarrels.

He that goes to bed thirsty riseth healthy.

Who will make a door of gold must knock a nail everyday.

A trade is better than service.

He that lives in hope danceth without music.

To review one's store is to mow twice.

Saint Luke was a saint and a physician, yet is dead.

Without business, debauchery.

Without danger we cannot get beyond danger.

If gold knew what gold is, gold would get gold, I wis.

Health and sickness are men's double enemies.

Little losses amaze, great tame.

Choose none for thy servants who have served thy betters.

Service without reward is punishment.

If the husband be not at home, there is nobody.

An oath that is not to be made is not to be kept.

The eye is bigger than the belly.

If you would be at ease, all the world is not.

Were it not for the bone in the leg, all the world would turn carpenters (to make them crutches).

If you must fly, fly well.

All that shakes falls not.

All beasts of prey are strong or treacherous.

If the brain sows not corn, it plants thistles.

A man well mounted is ever choleric.

Every one is a master and servant.

A piece of a church-yard fits every body.

One mouth doth nothing without another.

A master of straw eats a servant of steel.

An old cat sports not with her prey.

A woman conceals what she knows not.

He that wipes the child's nose kisseth the mother's cheek.

Gentility is nothing but ancient riches.

To go upon the Franciscans' hackney; *i.e.* on foot.

Amiens was taken by the fox, and retaken by the lion.

After death the doctor.

Ready money is a ready medicine.

It is the philosophy of the distaff.

It is a sheep of Beery, it is marked on the nose: applied to those that have a blow.

To build castles in Spain.

An idle youth, a needy age.

Silk doth quench the fire in the kitchen.

The words ending in "*ique*" do mock the physician; as hectique, paralitique, apoplectique, lethargique.

He that trusts much obliges much, says the Spaniard.

He that thinks amiss concludes worse.

A man would live in Italy (a place of pleasure), but he would choose to die in Spain (where they say the Catholic religion is professed with greatest strictness).

Whatsoever was the father of a disease, an ill diet was the mother.

Frenzy, heresy, and jealousy, seldom cured.

There is no heat of affection but is joined with some idleness of brain, says the Spaniard.

The war is not done so long as my enemy lives.

Some evils are cured by contempt.

Power seldom grows old at court.

Danger itself is the best remedy for danger.

Favour will as surely perish as life.

Fear the beadle of the law.

Heresy is the school of pride.

For the same man to be a heretic and a good
    subject is impossible.

Heresy may be easier kept out than shook off.

Infants' manners are moulded more by the example
    of parents than by stars at their nativities.

They favour learning whose actions are worthy of a
    learned pen.

Modesty sets off one newly come to honour.

No naked man is sought after to be rifled.

There is no such conquering weapon as the necessity
    of conquering.

Nothing secure unless suspected.

No tie can oblige the perfidious.

Spies are the ears and eyes of princes.

The life of spies is to know, not be known.

Religion a stalking horse to shoot other fowl.

It is a dangerous fire begins in the bed straw.

Covetousness breaks the bag.

Fear keeps and looks to the vineyard, and not the
    owner.

The noise is greater than the nuts.

Two sparrows on one ear of corn make an ill agree-
    ment.

The world is now a-days, God save the conqueror.

Unsound minds, like unsound bodies, if you feed,
    you poison.

Not only ought fortune to be pictured on a wheel,
    but everything else in this world.

All covet, all lose.

Better is one *Accipe*, than twice to say, *Dabo tibi*.

An ass endures his burden, but not more than his
burden.

Threatened men eat bread, says the Spaniard.

The beads in the hand, and the devil in capuch; or
cape of the cloak.

He that will do thee a good turn, either he will be
gone or die.

I escaped the thunder, and fell into the lightning.

A man of a great memory without learning hath a
rock and a spindle, and no staff to spin.

The death of wolves is the safety of the sheep.

He that is once born once must die.

He that hath but one eye must be afraid to lose it.

He that makes himself a sheep shall be eat by the
wolf.

He that steals an egg will steal an ox.

He that will be surety shall pay.

He that is afraid of leaves goes not to the wood.

In the mouth of a bad dog falls often a good bone.

Those that God loves do not live long.

Still fisheth he that catcheth one.

All flesh is not venison.

A city that parleys is half gotten.

A dead bee makes no honey.

An old dog barks not in vain.

They that hold the greatest farms pay the least rent:
(applied to rich men that are unthankful to God).

Old camels carry young camels' skins to the market.

He that hath time and looks for better time, time
comes that he repents himself of time.

Words and feathers the wind carries away.

Of a pig's tail you can never make a good shaft.

The bath of the blackamoor hath sworn not to whiten.

To a greedy eating horse a short halter.

The devil divides the world between atheism and
superstition.

Such a saint, such an offering.
We do it soon enough, if that we do be well.
Cruelty is more cruel, if we defer the pain.
What one day gives us another takes away from us.
To seek in a sheep five feet when there are but four.
A scabbed horse cannot abide the comb.
God strikes with His finger, and not with all His arm.
God gives His wrath by weight, and without weight His mercy.
Of a new prince new bondage.
New things are fair.
Fortune to one is mother, to another is stepmother.
There is no man, though never so little, but sometimes he can hurt.
The horse that draws after him his halter is not altogether escaped.
We must recoil a little, to the end we may leap the better.
No love is foul nor prison fair.
No day so clear but hath dark clouds.
No hare so small but hath his shadow.
A wolf will never make war against another wolf.
We must love as looking one day to hate.
It is good to have some friends both in heaven and hell.
It is very hard to shave an egg.
It is good to hold the ass by the bridle.
The healthful man can give counsel to the sick.
The death of a young wolf doth never come too soon.
The rage of a wild boar is able to spoil more than one wood.
Virtue flies from the heart of a mercenary man.
The wolf eats oft of the sheep that have been warned.
The mouse that hath but one hole is quickly taken.
To play at chess when the house is on fire.
The itch of disputing is the scab of the church.

Follow not truth too near the heels, lest it dash out thy teeth.

Either wealth is much increased, or moderation is much decayed.

Say to pleasure, Gentle *Eve*, I will none of your apple.

When war begins, then hell openeth.

There is a remedy for everything, could men find it.

There is an hour wherein a man might be happy all his life could he find it.

Great fortune brings with it great misfortune.

A fair day in winter is the mother of a storm.

Woe be to him that reads but one book.

Tithe, and be rich.

Take heed of
- The wrath of a mighty man, and the tumult of the people.
- Mad folks in a narrow place.
- Credit decayed and people that have nothing.
- A young wench, a prophetess, and a Latin-bred woman.
- A person marked, and a widow thrice married.
- Foul dirty ways and long sickness.
- Wind that comes in at a hole and a reconciled enemy.
- A step-mother; the very name of her sufficeth.

Princes are venison in heaven.

Critics are like brushers of noblemen's clothes.

He is a great necromancer, for he asks counsel of the dead: *i.e.* books.

A man is known to be mortal by two things, sleep and lust.

Love without end, hath no end, says the Spaniard: meaning, if it were not begun on particular ends it would last.

Stay awhile that we may make an end the sooner.

Presents of love fear not to be ill taken of strangers.

To seek these things is lost labour: geese in an oil pot,
  fat hogs among Jews, and wine in a fishing net.
Some men plant an opinion they seem to eradicate.
The philosophy of princes is to dive into the secrets
  of men, leaving the secrets of nature to those
  that have spare time.
States have their conversions and periods as well
  as natural bodies.
Great deservers grow intolerable presumers.
The love of money and the love of learning rarely meet.
Trust no friend with that you need, fear him as if
  he were your enemy.
Some had rather lose their friend than their jest.
Marry your daughters betimes lest they marry
  themselves.
Soldiers in peace are like chimneys in summer.
Here is a talk of the Turk and the pope, but my
  next neighbour doth me more harm than either
  of them both.
Civil wars of *France* make a million of atheists and
  thirty thousand witches.
We bachelors laugh and show our teeth, but you
  married men laugh till your hearts ache.
The devil never assails a man except he find him
  either void of knowledge, or of the fear of God.
There is nobody will go to hell for company.
Much money makes a country poor, for it sets a
  dearer price on everything.
The virtue of a coward is suspicion.
A man's destiny is always dark.
Every man's censure is first moulded in his own
  nature.
Money wants no followers.
Your thoughts close and your countenance loose.
Whatever is made by the hand of man, by the hand
  of man may be overturned.